# Plato's Menexenus and Pericles' Funeral Oration

## Empire and the Ends of Politics

# Plato's Menexenus and Pericles' Funeral Oration

## Empire and the Ends of Politics

Susan D. Collins
Southern Illinois University
Devin Stauffer
Kenyon College

Focus Classical Library
Focus Publishing/R Pullins Company
Newburyport MA 01950

The Focus Classical Library
Series Editors • James Clauss • Michael Halleran • Albert Keith Whitaker

Hesiod's *Theogony* • Richard Caldwell • 1987
*The Heracles* of Euripides • Michael Halleran • 1988
Aristophanes' *Lysistrata* • Jeffrey Henderson • 1988
Sophocles' *Oedipus at Colonus* • Mary Whitlock Blundell • 1990
Euripides' *Medea* • Anthony Podlecki • 1991
Aristophanes' *Acharnians* • Jeffrey Henderson • 1992
Aristophanes' *The Clouds* • Jeffrey Henderson • 1992
*The Homeric Hymns* • Susan Shelmerdine • 1995
Aristophanes: *Acharnians, Lysistrata, Clouds* • Jeffrey Henderson • 1997
Euripides' *Bacchae* • Stephen Esposito • 1998
Terence: *Brothers* • Charles Mercier • 1998
Sophocles' *Antigone* • Mary Whitlock Blundell • 1998

The Focus Philosophical Library
Series Editor • Albert Keith Whitaker

Plato's *Sophist* • E. Brann, P. Kalkavage, E. Salem • 1996
Plato's *Parmenides* • Albert Keith Whitaker • 1996
Plato's *Symposium* • Avi Sharon • 1998
Plato's *Phaedo* • E. Brann, P. Kalkavage, E. Salem • 1998
Plato's *Menexenus* & Pericles' Funeral Oration • S.D. Collins, D. Stauffer • 1999

ISBN 0-941051-70-6

Cover Design: Catherine Dripps

Printed in the United States of America
10 9 8 7 6 5 4 3 2 1

# CONTENTS

Introduction ........................................................................................ 1

Translators' Note ............................................................................... 20

Select Bibliography .......................................................................... 21

Pericles' Funeral Oration (II.35-46) ............................................. 23

Plato's Menexenus ............................................................................ 33

# INTRODUCTION

This volume brings together two works of classical antiquity, Pericles' Funeral Oration from Thucydides' history of the Peloponnesian War and Plato's *Menexenus*. The first of these works is well-known and widely studied, and thus requires little introduction; but the second, though from the pen of an author no less renowned, has never achieved similar prominence. That the *Menexenus* should suffer such neglect is surprising, for Plato is famous for his political dialogues—such as the *Republic* and the *Laws*—and the *Menexenus* is nothing if not political. But the neglect of the *Menexenus* seems to have been due in no small part to its strange and unfamiliar depiction of Socrates and the seemingly un-Platonic approach it takes to its political theme. Whereas in the *Republic* and the *Laws*, for instance, political questions are clearly approached from the perspective of philosophy—with Socrates (or his stand-in, the Athenian Stranger) engaging various interlocutors in a dialectical investigation of moral and political questions posed in broad or universal terms—in the *Menexenus* Socrates is cast in a truly unusual role: aside from a brief conversation with the young Menexenus at the beginning of the dialogue and an even briefer one at the end, Socrates appears not as a dialectician but as a rhetorician delivering a statesmanlike speech which he says could be given to the Athens of his day. Moreover, the perspective of the dialogue is mainly practical, not theoretical: Socrates' speech is a funeral oration delivered at the end of the Corinthian War (386 B.C.), and in the tradition of such orations, its author seeks to justify the deaths of Athenian citizens in battle by an encomium of the city for which they died.[1] As a result of these anomalies, the *Menexenus*

---

[1]   The most extensive study of the Athenian funeral oration as a genre of its own and as a distinctive Athenian institution is Nicole Loraux's *The Invention of Athens: The Funeral Oration in the Classical City*, translated by Alan Sheridan (Cambridge, MA: Harvard University Press, 1986). See also John Ziolkowski's *Thucydides and the Tradition of Funeral Speeches at Athens* (New York: Arno Press, 1981). See Thucydides II.34 for an account of the funeral ceremony.

1

does not rise to the dizzying heights or possess the grand sweep of Plato's other political dialogues. Yet for this very reason, it is perplexing. Even the eminent scholar Paul Friedländer begins his treatment of the dialogue by expressing bafflement: "This is Plato's most confusing work and, among his numerous portraits of Socrates, it is the most paradoxical."[2] And Charles Kahn emphatically concurs: "This little work is almost certainly the most enigmatic of all Plato's writings."[3] What then are we to make of the *Menexenus*? Why do we find Socrates, the famous philosopher and self-proclaimed civic gadfly, praising his city to the skies and exhorting his fellow citizens with a long speech in place of his typical—and critical—dialectics?

The main aim of our introduction to the following translations is to cap-ture the value and appeal of studying the *Menexenus*, especially in juxtapo-sition to Pericles' famous celebration of imperial politics in his Funeral Oration. We think that a comparison of these two works can provide a unique window on a number of great and enduring questions of politics: How should a city or a nation conduct itself in its relations with other cit-ies? What is the proper relation between foreign and domestic affairs? What are the proper ends of political life? On questions such as these—as well as on that most famous of Platonic themes, the relation of politics to philoso-phy—the comparison proposed by this volume, and encouraged by the *Menexenus* itself, can be of much interest. Since the *Menexenus* is such a strange and generally unknown dialogue, however, we shall begin by try-ing to provide some preliminary acquaintance with its more peculiar fea-tures.

The *Menexenus* presents a conversation between Socrates and his young friend Menexenus, and the most immediate difficulty that confronts the reader is to try to gauge just how seriously he or she ought to take this conversation. This difficulty arises because the funeral oration that is the

---

2    *Plato II: The Dialogues*, translated by Hans Meyerhoff (London: Routledge & Kegan Paul, 1964), p. 216.

3    "Plato's Funeral Oration: The Motive of the *Menexenus*," *Classical Philol-ogy* 58 (October 1963), p. 220. The dialogue has so puzzled readers as to compel some to argue that it is spurious. See Eduard Zeller, *Platonische Studien* (Tübingen: C.F. Osiander, 1839), p. 146; see also Schleiermacher's disparaging comments in *Schleiermacher's Introductions to the Dialogues of Plato*, translated by William Dobson (Cambridge, MA: J. & J. Deighton, 1836), pp. 337-341. For the authenticity of the *Menexenus*, however, we have the testimony of Aristotle, who alludes twice to the dialogue in his *Rhetoric* (at 1367b and 1415b), as well as other reliable sources, such as Ariston of Keos (the fourth successor to the head of Aristotle's Lyceum), Cicero, and Dionysius of Halicarnasus. See Robert Clavaud, *Le "Ménexène" de Platon et la rhétorique de son temps* (Paris: Belles Lettres, 1980), pp. 17-29.

centerpiece of the dialogue, a speech which is intended for a somber occasion and not without its moving passages, is combined with a comedy worthy of Aristophanes. For instance, only the most humorless reader could take seriously Socrates' claim to his unconvinced young friend that he learned the funeral oration he recites in the *Menexenus* from Pericles' mistress, Aspasia—a speechwriter of such talents that Socrates surmises she must have written Pericles' speech as well! These remarks occur, moreover, in the playful, friendly conversation between Socrates and Menexenus which opens the dialogue: upon learning that Menexenus is returning from the Chamber of the Athenian Council where he had gone to observe the selection of a funeral speaker, Socrates first teases the young man for his political ambitions and then proceeds to heap abuse on the Athenian orators and their flattering funeral orations. When this provokes a challenge from Menexenus, Socrates next claims that he too could succeed in such an arena by giving the speech of Aspasia—a speech which itself proves to contain its fair share of comedy or ridiculousness, including a long history of Athenian actions in war riddled with distortions and ending with the peace of Antalcidas, some 12 years after Socrates' own death. With Socrates speaking from the grave, and not exactly giving the whole truth and nothing but the truth, it is not surprising that many have been led to the conclusion that the *Menexenus* is meant as a parody or a lampoon.[4] But even if one is tempted by this reading, what is one to make of the fact that Socrates' funeral oration culminates in moving addresses to the children and parents of the fallen Athenians which seem undeniably serious and grave? This part of Socrates' speech, at the very least, cannot be laughed off as comic. And as for the speech as a whole, it is certainly worth noting that Menexenus himself—however incredulous he is that Socrates learned it from Aspasia—concludes the dialogue by expressing his admiration of the speech and his gratitude to Socrates for having delivered it.

So, despite its many jokes, it seems impossible to say that the *Menexenus* is simply a farce. But what then is its purpose? Why did Plato write such a dialogue? The best way of approaching this question, we think, is to follow the hint Socrates himself offers and to read the dialogue as directed against Pericles' Funeral Oration. In fact, it is an understatement to say that Socrates offers a "hint" that Pericles is his target. Not only does Socrates attribute his speech to Pericles' mistress Aspasia, but he even claims that his speech is composed, at least in part, of "leftovers" that Aspasia had lying around

---

4    See, e.g., Loraux, *Invention*, pp. 304-327; M.M. Henderson, "Plato's *Menexenus* and the Distortion of History," *Acta Classica*, 18 (1975), pp. 25-46; E.R. Dobbs, "Plato's *Gorgias*" (Oxford: Clarendon University Press, 1959), p. 24. For a more thorough survey of the main controversies in the interpretation of the *Menexenus*, see Clavaud's *Le "Ménexène" de Platon*.

from the time when she (supposedly) composed Pericles' speech, that is, of scraps that she cut out of that original speech (236b). While it goes without saying that these remarks should be taken with the proper grain of salt, they are nevertheless as direct an indication as one is likely to get in a Platonic dialogue that one should have Pericles' speech in the other hand when reading Socrates'.

Beyond this direct though admittedly comic indication that Pericles is Socrates' primary target in the *Menexenus*, there is of course also the broader evidence provided by the form of the dialogue—again, the greater part of the *Menexenus* is itself a funeral oration—as well as by its most obvious topic: Athens. In his speech, Socrates presents a portrait of Athens' origins, character, and above all her history which calls out to be compared with the celebrated portrait of the city drawn by Pericles. In the remainder of this introduction, accordingly, we shall try to take the first steps in this direction. Our intention in what follows is by no means to offer a complete interpretation of either work. Rather, by bringing out and reflecting upon a few of the highlights in Socrates' and Pericles' respective presentations of Athens, we hope simply to indicate the main lines of disagreement between Socrates and Pericles, most significantly their disagreement over the end to which Athens, or indeed any political community, ought to be devoted. This, then, is our primary aim; but it will ultimately lead us to spell out what we believe to be the deepest riddle of the *Menexenus*, the one which lies behind the dialogue's more manifest riddles. To state it briefly, this deepest riddle is that the "Socratic politics" that is presented in the *Menexenus*—a politics which will come to sight as remarkably more restrained and traditional than the politics of Pericles—would appear to be at significant odds with the activity of Socratic philosophy. We shall therefore conclude this introduction by considering whether, even from the perspective of the Socrates with whom we are most familiar, the restrained and traditional Athens depicted in the *Menexenus* is still to be preferred over her more glamorous Periclean twin.

## Pericles' Imperial Athens
## and Socrates' Revision of History

To compare Socrates' speech in the *Menexenus* with Pericles' Funeral Oration is to compare it, of course, with the most famous expression of Athens' self-understanding at the height of her imperial power. Pericles' memorable depiction of Athens' unique practices, regime, and ways (see II.36.4),[5] and especially of the unique marriage in Athens of freedom and

---

5    Further references to Pericles' Funeral Oration will include only the section numbers. Every other reference to Thucydides will include the book number in Roman numerals.

virtue, has as its peak a portrait of Athens in her imperial greatness. And this portrait is rightly famous for the grandeurs of its claims: Pericles praises the Athenian empire as the highest expression of human striving and as a goal in which human beings can find their full satisfaction.[6]

The pride of place Pericles accords the empire is reflected in the plan of his speech. After giving a brief account of Athens' origins and cursory honor to the older generations of Athenians, whose virtue kept Athens free from foreign domination (36.1-2), Pericles awards the highest honors to his own generation, who extended or "augmented" the empire, "equipping the city in every way to be most self-sufficient in both war and peace" (36.3). It is on this imperial generation that Pericles focuses throughout his speech, first in sketching the domestic arrangements and mores that have made Athenian imperialism possible (37.1 - 41.1), and then in describing the character of this imperialism itself (41.2 - 43.6). The empire, according to Pericles, is both a testimony to and the arena for the virtue of the Athenians (41.2).[7] In his description of Athenian imperialism, however, it is striking that Pericles does not single-out any particular actions or battles in which individual Athenians displayed their virtue. Rather than praising, for instance, the men who fought at Corcyra or Potidaea, he portrays Athens as a whole greater than its parts and almost as if she were a separate being capable of action of her own, declaring: "*our city* alone of the current powers proves when tested to be superior to what is said of her, and *she alone* gives no grounds for her attackers to be vexed about the sort of people by whom they have been harmed, or for her subjects to complain that they are being ruled by those who are unworthy" (41.3, italics added). Similarly, even in those instances in which Pericles speaks not simply of imperial Athens but of the imperial Athenians, it is notably as a collective, as "we": "leaving great monuments and securing a power that is not without witness, *we* shall be marveled at by our contemporaries as well as those to come, and *we* have no need in addition of praise from a Homer"; "*we* have compelled every sea and land to become a pathway for our daring, and have everywhere established everlasting memorials of deeds bad and good" (41.4, italics added).

---

6    See W.R. Connor, *Thucydides* (Princeton: Princeton University Press, 1984), pp. 66, 73-74; Clifford Orwin, *The Humanity of Thucydides* (Princeton: Princeton University Press, 1994), pp. 15, 20.

7    See Jacqueline de Romilly, *Thucydides and Athenian Imperialism*, translated by Philip Thody (Oxford: Basil Blackwell, 1963), p. 131: "[Athens'] power is considered only as the result (and, on this occasion, the proof) of the Athenian merits which have been analyzed in the speech as a whole. This power owes its existence to the principles on which Athens acts, to her political habits and to her way of life in general; it follows from what might be called her spiritual superiority." See also Connor, *Thucydides*, p. 66.

In keeping with this effort to direct the Athenians' gaze to the power and greatness of their city viewed as a whole, Pericles' praise of the empire culminates in an exhortation of the individual Athenians to lose themselves in their love of Athens, of Athens precisely in her imperial splendor (43.1). Pericles is emphatic in portraying this splendor and the willingness of the Athenians to devote themselves to it as noble, by which he means first and foremost that it transcends mere "calculation of advantage" (see especially 40.5 and 43.1).[8] Furthermore, since the noblest actions can be found only in the risks taken on behalf of empire, Pericles elevates courage and daring above all the other virtues and urges his fellow Athenians to emulate the manliness of those who lost their lives by facing such risks (41.1-6). Nevertheless, Pericles does not exhaust his exhortation of the Athenians with his appeal to courage and nobility. Even as he calls for the Athenians to undertake and endure courageously the "noblest of risks," and in doing so to consign all their other longings to hope, Pericles also holds out the promise that by dying with "their fame rather than their fear at its peak," they will achieve the only good truly worth having: "ageless praise" (43.2).[9] By losing themselves in a love of Athens and by nobly offering up their lives on her behalf, the Athenians, Pericles promises, will each find his own true happiness. Thus Pericles urges them to equate happiness with courage—"judge happiness to be freedom, and freedom to be courage"—and it is in this spirit that he commands them not to pause before the dangers of war (43.4). According to Pericles' full view, then, Athens is great and noble not only because of the extent of her rule and the magnitude of her power, but also because her great empire makes possible the noblest and best life for a human being.

From the heights of Pericles' portrayal of imperial Athens, the Athens that Socrates presents in the *Menexenus* appears much less brilliant and even small. It also appears much more respectful of ancestral traditions. Whereas Pericles moves quickly in his speech to his own imperial generation, leaving behind the older generation of Athenian ancestors and even the preceding generation of "our fathers" (36.1-3), Socrates begins from a

---

8    See David Bolotin, "Thucydides" in *History of Political Philosophy*, 3rd. edition, edited by Leo Strauss and Joseph Cropsey (Chicago: University of Chicago Press, 1986), p. 20. We are following Orwin, *Humanity of Thucydides*, p. 17, n. 4 in reading section 40 in general and 40.4-5 in particular as referring to the Athenian empire (cf. Simon Hornblower, *A Commentary on Thucydides*, volume 1 [Oxford: Clarendon Press, 1991], p. 305, and J.S. Rusten, *Thucydides Book Two* [Cambridge: Cambridge University Press, 1989], p. 156).

9    Rusten (*Thucydides Book Two*, pp. 161-162) observes that Pericles' description of the decision made by the fallen soldiers also serves as an exhortation of the living, and that this exhortation does not simply call the Athenians to sacrifice but offers glory as a great reward. See also Romilly, *Thucydides and Athenian Imperialism*, pp. 138-139 and Connor, *Thucydides*, pp. 73-74.

long and strange account of the origin of Athens. Claiming that the Athenians grew from their own mother earth (237b-238b; cf. *Republic* 414d-415a), he is at pains to stress the debt of gratitude and reverence the Athenians owe not only to their mother earth and their ancestors but also to the gods who "established our way of life" (238b). After this, Socrates proceeds to the Athenian regime, describing it as the "nurturer" and "educator" responsible for the Athenians' goodness and as an aristocracy with a long history of "kings" (238b-239a).[10] This description of the Athenian regime is followed in turn by Socrates' extended history of the Athenians at war (239a-246a).

It is in this third section of his speech that Socrates' account of the Athenians most obviously diverges from that of Pericles. Against the ranking implicit in Pericles' rapid ascent from more distant ancestors to "our fathers" to his own generation, a ranking reflecting Pericles' estimation of the Athenian empire and dictating his emphasis on recent deeds, Socrates awards the highest honors in his speech, the "top prizes," to the old heroes of the Persian Wars and above all to those who scored the first victory over the Persians at Marathon (240b-241a). These men, he stresses, were not aggressors; quite the contrary, they fought to defend the safety and freedom of the Greeks (239a-b, 240e), and this they did out of the belief not that war itself is something noble but only that it is sometimes necessary (239b).

Claiming that the deed at Marathon became the model for all subsequent generations of Athenians—that they became "students of those at Marathon" (240e)—Socrates then goes on to describe the *entire* history of Athens as characterized by the defense of safety and freedom. Astonishingly, Socrates' history of Athens at war *makes no mention of Athenian imperialism.* This incredible omission requires more than a little fancy footwork on Socrates' part. For instance, he describes the period of Athenian history most conspicuous for the rise of the Athenian empire (the early fifth century) as if it were nothing more than the final prosecution of the Persian Wars; saying not a word about Athenian aggression against Greeks during this time, Socrates speaks only of how the Athenians "cleared away the whole Barbarian force and drove it off the sea" (241d). He also gives a muted and dubious account of the great activity and fervor that preceded the Peloponnesian War. This crucial period, which saw the Greeks lining up against each other in alliance with either Athens or Sparta, Socrates de-

---

[10]   Compare Thucydides 37.1-2. On Socrates' account of the Athenian regime in general, and in particular on the meaning of Socrates' claim that it is an aristocracy, see Stephen Salkever, "Socrates' Aspasian Oration: The Play of Philosophy and Politics in Plato's *Menexenus*," *American Political Science Review* 87 (March 1993), p. 138. See also Kahn, "The Motive of the *Menexenus*," pp. 225-226, and Gregory Vlastos, *Platonic Studies* (Princeton: Princeton University Press, 1981), pp. 192-201.

scribes only as a time of peace which then gave way to hostilities and eventually to war when the other Greeks' "emulation" of Athens' success turned to "envy" (242a; cf. Thucydides I.89-118; see also II.64.3-5).[11] Now, if one judges only by what he says and not by what he omits, there may be some truth to Socrates' account of the fifth century: the line dividing Athens' assertive but welcomed leadership in ridding Greece of the Persian threat and her own imperial aggression is not a simple one to draw, and the animosity of the other Greeks towards Athens may indeed have had some root in envy. Yet by speaking only of envy as the cause of the Peloponnesian War, Socrates leaves out, at the very least, the role that was surely played by hatred and especially by fear of Athenian expansion and of the aggressive Athenian military.[12] Indeed, in limiting his explanation to a change in the minds or hearts of the other Greeks—from emulation to envy—Socrates leaves out any change that may have occurred within the Athenians themselves, that is, any rise of imperial ambitions. In what is only the most farfetched example of the lengths to which this requires Socrates to go, he claims that the Sicilian expedition—an expedition fueled in Thucydides' description by imperial longings so strong as to be called a form of "love" (see VI.24)—was simply another demonstration of Athens' commitment to the defense of freedom, this time the freedom of the Leontinians (242e-243a).

But what does all this add up to? Most simply stated, Socrates' silence about Athenian imperialism, and more generally his attempt to portray the entire history of Athens as guided by nothing other than the defense of security and freedom, amounts to a very large lie.[13] Yet to note this, as many

---

[11]    See also Donald Kagan, *Pericles of Athens and the Birth of Democracy* (New York: Free Press, 1991), pp. 93-95.

[12]    Compare Thucydides: "The truest cause [of the Peloponnesian War], even if the one least apparent in speech, I believe to be that the Athenians by becoming great and instilling fear in the Lacedaemonians compelled them to make war" (I.23.6).

[13]    Socrates' silence about Athenian imperialism is perhaps the biggest distortion in an historical account that has no shortage of distortions or lies. For instance, Socrates also portrays the Athenians as *the* leaders of the Greeks in the Persian Wars, downplaying the role of the Spartans by making no mention of Thermopylae and by suggesting that Athens fought alone at Salamis and Artemesium; he declares, remarkably, that the Peloponnesian War ended in Athenian victory not defeat, claiming that Athens was undone only subsequently by civil war at home; and he obscures and misrepresents the alliance between Athens and Persia in the Corinthian War. For more thorough discussions of the distortions and lies in Socrates' account of Athenian history, see Kahn, "The Motive of the *Menexenus*," pp. 224-225; Méridier, *Platon Oeuvres*, pp. 59-64; Henderson, "Plato's *Menexenus* and the Distortion of History," pp. 38-46; and J.A. Shawyer, *The "Menexenus" of Plato* (Oxford: Clarendon Press, 1906), pp. xi-xv.

have, only raises an obvious question. Why does Socrates tell such a lie? The most immediate answer to this question, we think, comes to sight when Socrates' speech is set against the backdrop of Pericles' speech. For in contrast to Pericles' lavish praise of Athenian imperialism, Socrates' silence about the empire and the more incredible aspects of his "history" prove to be in the service of a kind of rededication of Athens to the cause for which the old heroes fought and died at Marathon: the freedom of the Athenians and the rest of the Greeks from domination and slavery. By whitewashing the empire and repainting Athens as a stalwart champion of Greek security and freedom, Socrates conceals the darker and uglier aspects of Athenian history, thereby condemning, if only by his silence, the conquest and subjugation of the Greeks for which Pericles applauds his own generation of Athenians. Reversing Pericles' emphasis, Socrates redirects the gaze of his fellow citizens to an earlier age whose heroes, famous as defenders of Greek freedom rather than despoilers of it, deserve the highest honors for their virtue. Still, it remains to ask why exactly Socrates should conceal and condemn that which Pericles most praises; what precisely is it that lies behind his effort to redraw the Periclean picture of Athens, a picture which is, after all, if not without its own exaggerations, surely the more accurate portrait of the city to which they both appeal?

We can begin to understand Socrates' effort by focusing on a concern that was most pressing for those who were victims of Athenian imperialism, but which Pericles himself tacitly dismisses: the concern for justice. In his exhortation to his fellow citizens, Pericles seems to recognize no compelling restrictions on Athens' pursuit of empire, not even such restrictions as might seem to be called for by the ties of kinship and proximity the various Greek cities had towards one another. Socrates, by contrast, recurs many times in his speech to the distinction between Greeks and Barbarians, maintaining not only that the natural and linguistic ties of kinship brought the Greeks together in common cause against the Persians, but also that these bonds ought to serve as a check against strife among the Greeks themselves (239a-b, 240e, 241a-c, 242a, 242d, 243b-c). In this sense at least, Socrates urges his fellow Athenians always to pursue the just course: to remain true to their oaths, and to defend those Greek cities threatened by enslavement while never themselves destroying or subjugating their neighbors (243e-244b, 245c-e). Pericles recognizes no such obligations. Quite the contrary, he explicitly classes the other Greeks alongside the Barbarians as enemies and goes so far as to characterize Athens' expansion after the Persian Wars as a kind of proving ground for the superiority of Athenian to Spartan virtue (36.4, 39.1-4). Perhaps the best summary of Pericles' attitude towards justice is his famous boast about the trail left by Athenian imperialism, his boast that Athens has "everywhere established everlasting memorials of deeds bad and good" (41.4).

But Socrates' defense of a more just foreign policy proves not to constitute his full response to Pericles. Indeed, given Pericles' explicit claims concerning the pursuit of empire, it is virtually incumbent upon Socrates to say more. For in urging the Athenians to devote themselves to the collective aim of empire, and even to sacrifice themselves on behalf of the city as a whole, Pericles claims that the actions taken on behalf of empire are the noblest and best actions both for the city and for each individual. Again, this is the spirit in which Pericles encourages his fellow citizens to emulate the virtue of those who have died fighting for Athens, and insists that it is only in the dangers of war that one may find one's true happiness. By contrast, Socrates' revision of history would seem to have the intended effect of encouraging the Athenians to reject the conviction that action in war is to be sought as an end in itself or as choiceworthy for its own sake. Socrates urges upon them, instead, the more moderate view that war is a means to the preservation of security and freedom. War, in other words, is rightly understood as a necessity which must sometimes be endured for the sake of preserving other, higher ends. Thus, whereas Pericles' view entails the subordination of private and domestic affairs to public and foreign ones, and ultimately of peace to war, the implication of Socrates' revision of Athenian history is that the relations are properly reversed: that is, in answer to one of the oldest questions of politics, and in opposition to Pericles, Socrates suggests that war is for the sake of peace, and not peace for the sake of war. Yet once we have posed the opposition between Socrates and Pericles in this way, we must then raise a further question at least about Socrates' position. For what is the basis of Socrates' elevation of peace and freedom over war and empire? If, as Pericles suggests, war is preferable to peace because actions in war are noblest and best, must not Socrates' preference for peace also be defended with a view to the actions it makes possible? In other words, does not a full response to Pericles yet require of Socrates an account of those actions or that way of life for the sake of which peace and freedom are to be cherished?

## Socrates' Alternative to the Periclean Way of Life

Insofar as the *Menexenus* provides an answer to this question and points to an end higher than war and for the sake of which peace and freedom are more choiceworthy, it comes in the final section of Socrates' speech. Having completed his account of Athenian actions in war, Socrates concludes by delivering messages to the children and parents of the dead (246c-249c). In these messages to the families, Socrates' funeral oration finds its most serious and solemn moment. By contrast, Pericles' speech reaches its high point in his praise of empire and his elevation of the city and deeds on her behalf as the highest and best object of Athenian devotion. When Pericles turns to address "those who remain," he has already drawn for them the lessons they ought to learn about what is noblest and best for the city and for a human being. His speech then descends from his encomium of empire to the lesser tasks of consolation and encouragement, reaching perhaps its lowest point in his infamous "brief piece of advice" to the widows (45.1).

But what, then, is the end or, more generally, the way of life that Socrates offers and advises against the Periclean view that the peak of virtue and the highest good can be achieved only in war and empire? As one might expect, this way of life is spelled out most clearly in Socrates' speech to the children, for they are the ones with the better part of their lives ahead of them and the ones most in need of education and guidance in such matters. Yet, while Socrates' advice comes where we might most expect it, the advice itself may be surprising. Famous for the view that philosophy is the best way of life and for exhorting others to philosophize, Socrates makes no mention of philosophy at this crucial point of the *Menexenus* but instead exhorts the children to the life of moral virtue as it is more conventionally understood. That is, against Pericles' radical praise of daring and unrestrained action in war, Socrates pits a more restrained and traditional view of virtue. Or rather, this must be qualified, for Socrates only reports such a view; strictly speaking, he gives no advice of his own. Telling the children that he will offer his own exhortation later— "whenever I meet one of you in the future, I shall remind you and urge you to strive eagerly to be as good as possible"[14]—Socrates now defers to another authority: "it is just that I tell you what your fathers, as they were about to risk their lives, solemnly enjoined us, should anything happen to them, to announce to those they would forever leave behind" (246c). To be sure, Socrates says that his message to the children from their fathers is composed only partly of their fathers' own words and includes additional things that he has inferred from what they used to say (246c). But Socrates admonishes the children that "you ought to believe that what I am reporting, you are hearing straight from them" (246c).

Speaking through Socrates, "the fathers" exhort their now-orphaned children to be virtuous. This includes, according to the fathers, being courageous in war, and they present themselves as exemplars of virtue for having chosen to risk their lives before bringing shame upon their families (246d). But importantly, the fathers do not restrict virtue to courageous action in war or even present such action as the peak of virtue. Rather,

---

[14]    Several commentators have noted here the allusion to the *Apology* 29d-30b. See, e.g., Friedländer, *Plato II*, p. 226; Henderson, "Plato's *Menexenus* and the Distortion of History," p. 45; and Coventry, "Philosophy and Rhetoric in the *Menexenus*," p. 14.

concerned less that their children prepare themselves to die nobly than that they equip themselves to live nobly, the fathers broaden the field of virtue and encourage their offspring to consider how they should conduct themselves in all their pursuits. "Even if you should practice something else," they urge the children, "practice it with virtue, knowing that without this all possessions and pursuits are shameful and base" (246e-247a). The fathers praise the whole of virtue, and if they single out any one virtue, it is less courage than justice: even "all knowledge" when "severed from justice and the rest of virtue, reveals itself as villainy not wisdom" (246e-247a). With regard to the virtuous life, the fathers do not simply hold themselves up as a model but challenge their offspring to try "in all things" and "in every way" to surpass their own accomplishments and even the accomplishments of their earlier ancestors.

Furthermore, if the fathers broaden the range of virtue in their exhortation to the children, they also wrap that exhortation in a tight web of ancestral, familial, and divine ties. They explain even their own choice to die as having been tied to a similar reflection concerning the consequences of acting ignobly, the reflection, namely, that for the one who has brought shame on his family, life is not worth living and that such a man will be left friendless both by men and by the gods. Several times in their address the fathers give the same caution to their own offspring, and, indeed, they conclude by admonishing the children not to "abuse or squander the reputation of your ancestors," and by leaving them with a final warning: "if you live by what we have said, you will come to us as friends to friends when your own fate carries you off. But if you are neglectful and live basely, no one will welcome you favorably" (247e). As the fathers' final warning indicates, the moral force of their exhortation to virtue is inseparable from familial attachments. It is all the more fitting, then, that Socrates should have stepped aside in this case—as Pericles does not—to let the voice of familial authority speak. When given its say, it brings to bear in support of virtue not only its own authority, but also the impressive weight of ancestral tradition and a reminder of the watchfulness of the gods.

Taking the fathers' speech to the children as our guide, then, we seem to have an answer to our question of the end or way of life that the *Menexenus* sets against Periclean imperialism and in light of which Socrates presents Athens as a city devoted in her foreign affairs to the defense of safety and freedom. This answer, in short, is the life of moral virtue. In fact, this life may supply an answer not only to the question of why peace and freedom are good—that is, what they are to be used for—but it may also help us to understand more fully why Socrates went to such lengths to hide Athenian imperialism. For since there is no absolute line between the principles that guide the conduct of foreign affairs and those that apply in the domestic sphere, the conduct of foreign affairs naturally has an impact on a city's domestic life. In its pursuit of great imperial actions abroad, the Athens of Pericles understands itself to be unrestricted by justice or any law that might limit its actions, and this very self-understanding would tend to foster a certain "liberation" from such restraints in its own citizens.[15] By contrast, the Athens Socrates presented earlier in his speech—a city rooted in the tradition of the Marathon fighters and always respectful of right—would provide both a model and a support for the observance of justice and the practice of virtue at home.

This is not to deny that Pericles' Athens, no less than the one Socrates presents, is also concerned to be virtuous. And it is true that Pericles presents the Athenian empire as noble, in this respect appealing to a moral concern in the Athenians—a concern to perform noble actions on a grand scale and to rise above private advantage in their devotion to a higher project. But as "moral" as Pericles' Athenian empire may be in one respect, we need only return to our earlier consideration of justice to see that it is also morally questionable. It was seen to be so, in fact, not only by its victims but also by some of the Athenians themselves, whom we find in Thucydides' history ready to interpret calamities like the plague and the great disaster at Sicily as deserved punishments for Athens' transgressions in her pursuit of empire (see Thucydides II.47, 53 and VII.77). Clearly, if Athenian imperialism elevated certain virtues, particularly the distinctive daring and courage for which Pericles praises the Athenians, it did so at the expense of defying those restrictions or laws—human and divine— that proscribe the unjust taking of power. Indeed, according to even Pericles himself, however noble the empire and however brilliant the daring of the men who acquired it, neither could ever shake the taint of injustice (see Thucydides II. 63). It is in recognition of this fact that in his final speech in Thucydides' history, Pericles characterizes the empire as a tyranny, acknowledging that it was unjust to have acquired it (II.63). Or does he ever really acknowledge this? Strictly speaking, what Pericles says in that speech is that the Athenians hold their empire *like* a tyranny which it *seems* (or "is held to be": *dokei*) unjust to have taken.[16] These qualifications may be Pericles' way of giving quiet voice to a perspective we find proclaimed more boldly by a number of other imperial Athenians in Thucydides, a perspective that understands Athenian imperialism to go hand in hand with a kind of self-proclaimed "moral enlightenment"—that is, with the view, given perhaps its most frank declaration by the infamous Athenian

---

[15]    For a fuller discussion of the impact of foreign policy—especially an imperial foreign policy—on domestic affairs, see Arlene Saxonhouse, "Nature and Convention in Thucydides' History," *Polity*, 10 (Summer, 1978), pp. 461-487.

[16]    See Orwin, *Humanity of Thucydides*, p. 21.

ambassadors to Melos, that appeals to justice are hollow words against those natural necessities which dictate the behavior of cities, and that the strong are not to blame for ceding to the irresistible temptation to seize power (V.89, 105; see also II.64). Nevertheless, while such "enlightenment" may have been essential to giving a justification of Athenian imperialism, or at least to quieting the qualms of its proponents, it is even more surely destructive of respect for the traditional supports—ancestral, familial, and divine—upon which Socrates relies so heavily in the fathers' speech to the children.[17] For all its supposed nobility, then, we can understand why Socrates objects to the imperialism celebrated by Pericles, since such imperialism ultimately seems to be a threat to moral virtue, undermining the fragile conditions of its practice and perhaps even leading some to lose belief in it altogether.

## The Paradox of Socrates' Conservatism

To this point our comparison of the *Menexenus* and Pericles' Funeral Oration has led us to the conclusion that Socrates' implicit objection to Pericles is an objection to his moral and political radicalism. Against this radicalism, Socrates pits a conservatism of moral restraint and respect for tradition. It is on these grounds, we suggest, that one might be able to make a certain sense even of the outlandish history of Athens presented by Socrates in the *Menexenus*. For as ridiculous as this presentation may be when considered as an accurate account of Athenian foreign policy, it is perhaps dictated by the kinds of concerns stressed in the message to the children, the one part of Socrates' speech which seems most undeniably serious. Nevertheless, as much as we may therefore be led to conclude that the Socrates of the *Menexenus* supports a more restrained and traditional politics as politically and morally healthy, it would be a mistake to be satisfied that this is Socrates' last word. In fact, the *Menexenus* itself gives us reasons to doubt this conclusion, or at least to wonder whether matters are not more complicated; and

[17]    Regarding Pericles' attitude towards the divine, consider the following statement of David Grene (*Man in his Pride* [Chicago: University of Chicago Press, 1950], p. 88), which refers to all three of Pericles' speeches in Thucydides: "It is extraordinary in such speeches as these—one contemplating the city's engagement in a long war, one spoken in praise of the dead, one defending a leader suspected because of what was accidental mischance—that, with the exception of one insignificant and quite colorless reference, there should be no mention of divine guidance, divine blessing, or even, in a merely sentimental allusion, fatherland's gods . . . [Pericles] shares with his hearers—knows it and draws his power from it—the knowledge that he and they are not like those of another age or another state who will bolster their hopes or their fears or even their sorrow by reference to beliefs outworn and dead." On "the amoral strain in Pericles' thought," see Connor, *Thucydides*, p. 75, n. 54.

the dialogue also points beyond its own text to other Platonic dialogues which should serve to increase our doubt.

The first and most obvious point which sets some distance between Socrates and the conservatism he appears to expound in the *Menexenus* is that he does not strictly speaking expound it himself: we must recall here that Socrates' exhortation to the children is not delivered in his own name. In this most solemn moment of his funeral oration, when Socrates exhorts the young to care for virtue out of filial piety, he steps aside and speaks as the voice of the children's fathers (246c). Indeed, if we recall that Socrates attributes his speech as a whole to Aspasia, he stands even at two removes from his advice to the children. Secondly, and perhaps of greater importance, the fathers' message to the children is only one of two messages Socrates delivers at the end of his speech. After addressing the children, Socrates delivers another message from the same dead to their mothers and fathers (247c-248d). Here too they offer advice—now as sons to parents—but in this advice they move a considerable distance from the view they were at such pains to stress to their children.

A sketch of only a few of the main points raised by a comparison of these two messages should suffice to indicate the significance of their striking differences, differences too great to be explained solely by the distinct requirements of exhorting the young and consoling the old. As one might expect, "the sons" attempt to console their parents by urging them to bear their loss as easily as possible. In support of this exhortation, however, they offer a rather remarkable interpretation of the famous Delphic proverb "Nothing too much." While it is surely in keeping with the spirit of the proverb that the sons underscore the importance of moderation, they carry this to an extreme by interpreting the Delphic saying as an injunction not to allow one's happiness to become overly dependent upon other human beings. They insist that he who "depends on himself for everything, or nearly everything, that brings happiness"—the man, that is, whose independence from other human beings protects his own fortunes from being "compelled to wander" with the changing fortunes of others—is the one who is "best prepared to live" (247e-248a). According to the sons, the one who achieves such self-sufficiency and independence is at once moderate, courageous, and prudent, and he is able to hold to the proverb's teaching even—indeed, most of all—under fortune's greatest turns: when his own children "come into being" or "perish," he will be found "neither taking joy nor grieving too much" (cf. *Republic* 387d-388a). As their unorthodox interpretation of the Delphic saying indicates, the sons' second message, while still a rejection of Periclean morality—here in the form of a preference for moderation over daring, and self-sufficiency over an erotic attachment to the city—also begins to depart from the earlier emphasis on the familial, the ancestral, and the divine. Their exhortation to become as independent as humanly possible obviously strains against their earlier admonitions to the children to be guided in their constant pursuit of virtue by a concern for familial and ancestral reputation and to keep in mind that they will find themselves friendless in the afterlife should they stray from the correct path. The sons' speech to the parents even takes on philosophic or "Socratic" overtones.[18] In urging their parents to seek self-sufficiency, the sons point toward an understanding of the virtues—with moderation, courage, and prudence all finding a common basis in self-sufficiency—that is more reminiscent of Socrates' famous dictum that virtue is knowledge than of the typical and traditional view of the virtues reflected in the warning to the children that all knowledge "when severed from justice and the rest of virtue" is villainy, not wisdom. It is in this latter message from the sons, too, that we find the first and only suggestion of a doubt in the *Menexenus* that the dead are able to perceive the living (248c). In short, this second message, in its movement away from the traditional ties and supports of civic life, begins to recall the more unconventional and controversial views we typically associate with Socrates.

The *Menexenus* provides one further indication that we should hesitate in taking Socrates' conservatism as his last word. This is the suggestion offered more broadly by the structure and drama of the dialogue as a whole. As we noted earlier, Socrates' long exhortatory speech is framed by two brief and playful exchanges with the young Menexenus. At the opening of the dialogue we find Socrates, having himself skipped the Athenian Council's planned selection of a funeral speaker, meeting Menexenus upon the latter's return from the Council-Chamber. Not uncharacteristically, Socrates wastes little time in chiding his young friend for taking such an ambitious interest in politics, and especially for his confidence that he has completed his education or studied enough philosophy and is ready now for what he appears to regard as the bigger and better task of ruling (234a-b, compare *Alcibiades I*).[19] In an effort to take some of the wind out of

---

18    Compare Salkever, "Socrates' Aspasian Oration," pp. 140-141; Friedländer, *Plato II*, pp. 226-227; Louis Méridier (editor), *Platon Oeuvres Complètes*, Tome V (Paris: Les Belles Lettres, 1931), pp. 71-72.

19    It is also worth noting that Socrates and Menexenus are speaking in private. Even if Socrates delivers a "public" speech in the *Menexenus*, he does not deliver it in public. Socrates' concern in the *Menexenus*, then, seems to be with a typically small (and typically young) audience—in this case an immediate audience of only one. However, whether Menexenus might not go on to report the speech to others, or to give it a more public airing, is an open question. Socrates' only injunction is that Menexenus not report him to Aspasia (see 249d-e). Cf. Salkever, "Socrates' Aspasian Oration," p. 136, and Arlene Saxonhouse, *Fear of Diversity: The Birth of Political Science in Ancient Greek Thought* (Chicago: University of Chicago Press, 1992), p. 117.

Menexenus' sails, Socrates ridicules here the solemn Athenian practice he himself goes on to imitate, the practice of delivering funeral orations: it is not hard to flatter Athenians, according to Socrates, especially if one is speaking before Athenians and willing to be a bit loose with the truth (234c-235d). This opening exchange, with its playful and conversational style, recalls the Socrates we know from Plato's other dialogues, and it serves as a warning that we must not forget the way Socrates spent most of his time. For as we are made well aware by Plato's other dialogues, Socrates was not disposed to spend the greater part of his day composing and delivering funeral orations. It is an exaggeration, but one Socrates himself encourages, to say that he spent virtually every waking moment questioning, examining (and doubting) the convictions of his fellow citizens. In contrast to his concern in the *Menexenus* that in reciting the funeral oration he will appear to be an old man playing like a child (236c), Socrates insists elsewhere that his investigations of the opinions of his fellow Athenians were the serious core of his otherwise playful life. As he puts it in Plato's *Apology*, these investigations—his famous (or infamous) eristical challenges to received opinion which we find captured so memorably in dialogues such as the *Republic*, the *Gorgias*, and the *Euthyphro*—were his business, not his leisure (*Apology* 23b-c). In fact, they were so much the focus of his life that Socrates says they left him no time to attend to the affairs of the city (see again, *Apology* 23b-c; but consider 38a and *Phaedo* 96a-100a).

It is especially when placed against the backdrop of his more characteristic philosophic activity that the Socrates of the body of the *Menexenus* becomes a riddle or an enigma. And we are thus returned to the paradox posed by the dialogue: that Socrates, best known as a dialectical critic of his fellow citizens, not to say as a gadfly who so disturbed Athens that she took the most extreme measure to quiet him, is transformed in the *Menexenus* into an orator who praises his city and its traditions—and who praises them, moreover, with a long speech in place of his typical questioning. If in his guise as a rhetorician in the *Menexenus* Socrates may appear conservative and traditional, that now seems another way of saying that he also appears un-Socratic. How are we to make sense, then, of Socrates' alliance with the city in the *Menexenus*, an alliance made all the more puzzling since it is with the city portrayed not in its Periclean openness and freedom but as closed and restrained? This is the problem, as we indicated at the beginning of this introduction, that we take to be at the core of the perplexing character of the *Menexenus* and its "paradoxical portrait of Socrates."

Now, it is difficult, we think, to resolve the paradox posed by the *Menexenus* on the basis of the *Menexenus* alone, for Plato provides us with only enough glimmers of Socrates the philosopher to raise the question of his relation to Socrates the rhetorician. It would also stray beyond the task of an introduction such as this to attempt to answer every question the dialogue raises. Nevertheless, having compared the *Menexenus* with Pericles' Funeral Oration, let us sketch the outlines of a possible resolution which presents itself when the *Menexenus* is read as Plato's response to Pericles and the politics that he praises. If this response suggests anything, it suggests that Plato took a critical view of the moral effects of such politics. And these effects he may have judged to be harmful not only on the plane of politics—the most obvious plane of his criticism—but also from the point of view of *philosophy itself*. Admittedly, this may seem like an odd suggestion, for isn't Socratic philosophizing, as we ourselves have just suggested, as radical as anything Pericles encourages? Yet it is important to consider not only the radical character of Socratic philosophizing but also its *prerequisites*. Socratic philosophy is most distinctive in its having the form of a dialectical ascent from the most serious attention to one's own deepest political convictions and opinions to an end, or a way of life, that may ultimately be transpolitical (consider *Republic* 514a-519b). (In this light, Socrates' oblivion to the Athenian Council's selection of the funeral speaker at the beginning of the *Menexenus* appears as a playful commentary on the ultimate priority of Socrates' own concerns.) Such an ascent, however, may depend for its possibility on the character of one's initial convictions, and on the seriousness or deep concern with which one approaches the very questions Socratic philosophy raises and examines—questions such as, to cite perhaps the two most central, "What is justice?" and "What is piety?" A deep concern for such matters would seem to be the necessary foundation of the pressing desire to know whether one's convictions about them are true, and thus to turning to Socratic philosophy in the first place.

From this point of view, then, it becomes possible to imagine a way in which Plato may have regarded Periclean politics as inimical even to philosophy itself. For, in contrast to the traditional and pious Athens praised by Socrates, the Athens of Pericles' Funeral Oration turns a blind eye on justice and the divine. As we have already stressed, Pericles pays little regard to justice in his famous encomium of the imperial city, and, except for a passing mention of sacrifices as a form of relaxation (38.1), he pays even less attention to the gods. Moreover, if we are struck by the radical character of Periclean politics, we should also be struck by the fact that what is most radical about it—the assumption that cities and individuals are free of any genuine restrictions or any higher authority—is given public sanction by Athens' greatest statesman. As a matter of public education, such a politics may weaken, not to say destroy, a serious concern on the part of its adherents with justice and piety, and thus with the questions pursued in the Socratic investigations. However paradoxical it may seem, this public education may thereby be an impediment to Socratic philosophy. The bold freedom proclaimed and preached by Pericles may encourage, especially in the young, a too easy confidence that they already know all they need to know about the most important questions—the kind of confidence for which Socrates teasingly chides Menexenus at the beginning of the dialogue, inferring from Menexenus' actions a belief that he is no longer in need of education or philosophy and now has nothing left to do but to rule over others (234a). Indeed, in this context, Socrates' observation may recall Pericles' sole reference to philosophy in his speech: his proud claim that the Athenians "philosophize without softness," a claim that is consistent with Pericles' elevation of war and imperial rule as the highest end of human life, and with his more general evaluation of the ultimate superiority and sufficiency of action, "deeds," over speech (40.1; see also 35.1, 41.2, 41.4). This is a ranking with which neither Plato nor his Socrates would agree. For through the model of Socrates and the Socratic life, Plato indicates clearly enough his own view that human life finds its peak not in political action, but in the philosophic activity, the "speeches," characteristic of Socrates (consider *Apology* 38a). The *Menexenus* may serve to remind and caution us, however, especially as we become drawn to Socratic philosophy, not to lose sight of the important difference between the prerequisites of such philosophizing and the activity itself. And if, as it seems, Socrates' own end in reciting the speech of Aspasia to his young, politically ambitious friend is to intervene in that friend's education, his recitation is thus a rare glimpse offered by Plato of the kind of education that is necessarily prior to philosophy.

# Translators' Note

The following translations are based upon the Oxford Classical Texts editions, *Thucydidis Historiae*, edited by Henry Stuart Jones (Oxford, 1942), and *Platonis Opera, III*, edited by John Burnet (Oxford, 1903). All deviations from these editions are noted. We wish to express our appreciation to A. Keith Whitaker, Robert C. Bartlett, and Joan O'Brien for their assistance and comments on various drafts of the translations, and to Gary Mullen for his help especially in compiling the historical notes to the *Menexenus*. A version of our introduction, which takes up the controversies in the secondary literature at greater length, appeared in *Review of Politics* 61 (Winter 1999), pp. 85-115, as "The Challenge of Plato's *Menexenus*."

We have tried to make our translations more literal than others that are available in order to give readers more direct access to the actual texts. Since our translations are almost entirely of orations, however, we thought it a mistake to strive for a word-for-word rendering of every passage. The efforts we have made to capture tone and style at the expense of literalness are nevertheless fairly minor, for we have preferred the difficult task of accuracy in translation to the impossible one of matching the rhetorical nuances of Thucydides' Pericles and Plato's Socrates.

# Select Bibliography

Below is a list of secondary sources we found helpful in studying the *Menexenus* and Pericles' Funeral Oration. The list is fairly complete for the *Menexenus* but contains only a small fraction of the vast literature on Thucydides.

Alfarabi. *Philosophy of Plato and Aristotle.* Translated by Muhsin Mahdi. New York: The Free Press, 1962.

Bolotin, David. "Thucydides," in *History of Political Philosophy*, 3rd. edition. Edited by Leo Strauss and Joseph Cropsey. Chicago: University of Chicago Press, 1986.

Clavaud, Robert. *Le "Ménexène" de Platon et la rhétorique de son temps.* Paris: Belles Lettres, 1980.

Connor, W.R. *Thucydides.* Princeton: Princeton University Press, 1984.

Coventry, Lucinda. "Philosophy and Rhetoric in the *Menexenus*," *Journal of Hellenic Studies* 109 (1989), pp. 1-15.

Dionysius of Halicarnasus. *Critical Essays.* Translated by Stephen Usher. Cambridge: Harvard University Press (Loeb Classical Library), 1974.

Dodds, E.R. *Plato's "Gorgias."* Oxford: Clarendon Press, 1959.

Friedländer, Paul. *Plato II: The Dialogues.* Translated by Hans Meyerhoff. London: Routledge & Kegan Paul, 1964.

Gomme, A.W. *A Historical Commentary on Thucydides.* Oxford: Clarendon Press, 1966.

Grene, David. *Man in His Pride.* Chicago: University of Chicago Press, 1950.

Henderson, M.M. "Plato's *Menexenus* and the Distortion of History," *Acta Classica* 18 (1975), pp. 25-46.

Hornblower, Simon. *A Commentary on Thucydides*, Volume 1. Oxford: Clarendon Press, 1991.

Huby, Pamela M. "The *Menexenus* Reconsidered," *Phronesis* 2 (1957), pp. 104-14.

Kagan, Donald. *Pericles of Athens and the Birth of Democracy.* New York: Free Press, 1991.

Kahn, Charles. "Plato's Funeral Oration: The Motive of the *Menexenus*," *Classical Philology* 58 (October, 1963), pp. 220-34.

Loraux, Nicole. "Socrate Contrepoison de L'Oraison Funèbre: Enjeu et signification du *Ménexène*," *L'antiquité classique* 43 (1974), pp. 172-211.

———. *The Invention of Athens: The Funeral Oration in the Classical City*. Translated by Alan Sheridan. Cambridge, MA: Harvard University Press, 1986.

Méridier, Louis (editor). *Platon Oeuvres Complètes*, Tome V. Paris: Les Belles Lettres (Budé Edition), 1931.

Monoson, S. Sara. "Remembering Pericles: The Political and Theoretical Import of Plato's *Menexenus*," *Political Theory* 26 (1998), pp. 489-513.

Orwin, Clifford. *The Humanity of Thucydides*. Princeton: Princeton University Press, 1994

Plutarch. *Lives*. Translated by John Dryden. New York: Modern Library, 1932.

Romilly, Jacqueline de. *Thucydides and Athenian Imperialism*. Translated by Philip Thody. Oxford: Basil Blackwell, 1963.

Rosenstock, Bruce. "Socrates as Revenant: A Reading of the *Menexenus*," *Phoenix* 48 (Winter, 1994), pp. 331-347.

Rusten, J.S. *Thucydides Book Two*. Cambridge: Cambridge University Press, 1989.

Salkever, Stephen. "Socrates' Aspasian Oration: The Play of Philosophy and Politics in Plato's *Menexenus*," *American Political Science Review* 87 (March, 1993), pp. 133-143.

Saxonhouse, Arlene W. "Nature & Convention in Thucydides' History," *Polity* 10 (Summer, 1978), pp. 461-487.

———. *Fear of Diversity: The Birth of Political Science in Ancient Greek Thought*. Chicago: University of Chicago Press, 1992.

Schleiermacher, Friedrich. *Schleiermacher's Introductions to the Dialogues of Plato*. Translated by William Dobson. Cambridge: J. & J.J. Deighton, 1836.

Shawyer, J.A. (editor). *The "Menexenus" of Plato*. Oxford: Clarendon Press, 1906.

Stern, Herald S. "Plato's Funeral Oration," *The New Scholasticism* 48 (Autumn, 1974), pp. 503-508.

Taylor, A.E. *Plato: The Man and His Works*. New York: Meridian Books, 1960.

Vlastos, Gregory. *Platonic Studies*. Princeton: Princeton University Press, 1981.

Zeller, Eduard. *Platonische Studien*. Tübingen: C.F. Osiander, 1839.

Ziolkowski, John E. *Thucydides and the Tradition of Funeral Speeches at Athens*. New York: Arno Press, 1981.

# PERICLES' FUNERAL ORATION
# (II.35-46)

35 (1) Many of those who have previously spoken here have praised the one who made this speech a part of our law,[1] saying that it is noble[2] that a speech be delivered over those being buried after falling in war. But I would have thought it enough that the honors of those who became good men[3] by deed be presented also by a deed—such as you see even now in what has been prepared at the public expense for this funeral—and not that belief in the virtue of many should be risked to one man's speaking well or badly.[4]

---

[1] *Nomos,* which we here and elsewhere translate as "law," has also the broader meaning of our word "custom." Pericles is likely not referring to a specific or written law but to the habitual practice of giving funeral orations which has thus become an established practice or custom. The funeral oration given here by Pericles occurs at the end of the first year of the Peloponnesian War, at which time the Athenians were still very much at the height of their power. (See Thucydides I.47 and 30, and note 1 to our introduction.)

[2] *Kalos* has a range of meanings including noble, beautiful, fine, fair, and good. No single English term can capture the full sense of the Greek, which expresses in one term what we distinguish by several and suggests that aesthetic and moral evaluations are not as separable as our linguistic distinctions seem to indicate. We always translate *kalos* in its various forms with the appropriate form of "noble"; cf. 35.1, 3, 42.4, 43.1. In one case, in which *kalos* appears as a part of the verb *philokalênai* (40.1), we translate it by its substantive "beauty," and in another case (41.5), we translate as "nobly" the adverbial form of *gennaios,* which denotes nobility conferred by high or good birth.

[3] *Andres agathoi genomenoi,* "who became good men," is a euphemistic way of referring to those who have died in battle. For the general absence of explicit references to death in the Athenian funeral orations, see Nicole Loraux, *The Invention of Athens: The Funeral Oration in the Classical City,* translated by Alan Sheridan (Cambridge, MA: Harvard University Press, 1986), pp. 2-3.

[4] Here, as throughout his speech, Pericles plays upon a juxtaposition of *logos* and *ergon.* We translate *logos* variously as "speech" or "reason," and *ergon* as "deed," "action," or "task" in accord with what seems appropriate or most graceful in the context. *Logismos,* which denotes more strictly "calculation," also appears twice, at 40.3 and 40.5, and a verbal form, *eklogizesthai,* appears at 40.3.

(2) For it is hard to speak with measure in a situation in which acceptance of the truth is secured only with great difficulty. The one listener, who is informed and of goodwill,[5] might believe that what is presented is wanting in comparison with what he wishes to hear and what he knows, while the other, who is uninformed, might believe out of envy that some things are even exaggerated, should he hear anything surpassing his own nature. For praise spoken of others is bearable only so long as each considers himself capable of any of the deeds of which he hears; if something outstrips them, they become envious and so at once distrustful. (3) Yet since such speeches were sanctioned as noble by the ancients, I too am bound, in keeping with the law, to try to meet the wishes and expectations of each of you, as far as that is possible.

36  (1) I shall begin with our ancestors, for it is just and also fitting on an occasion such as this that they be given this honor of remembrance. The same people always have inhabited our country and by their virtue have handed it down as free to generations successive to the present. (2) They are worthy of praise; and still more so are our fathers, who, in addition to what they inherited, acquired and bequeathed to us with no small toil as much of the empire as we now hold.[6] (3) But most parts of it we augmented— we ourselves who are here now and more or less in the prime of life—and we equipped the city in all ways to be most self-sufficient, in both war and peace.[7] (4) I shall leave aside the deeds in war by which each part was acquired—whether it was we or our fathers who ardently defended against an aggressive enemy,[8] Barbarian or Greek—for I do not wish to speak at length about these things before those who know.[9] But after first making clear through what sort of practices we have come to our present state and with what regime, and on account of what kind of ways our affairs have become great, I shall proceed to the praise of these here before us, in the belief that in the present circumstances it would not be unfitting for these things to be said and that it would

---

5    The goodwill of the listener is toward those spoken of.

6    Pericles refers to those who fought in the Persian Wars, the final prosecution of which was simultaneous with the birth of the Athenian empire. See Thucydides I.18.

7    As Pericles suggests, his own generation not so much enlarged the empire as shored up and strengthened what was already possessed.

8    Reading *polemion* with Haase instead of *polemos* with mss.

9    Pericles is passing over not only the events of the Persian Wars but also the events that led up to the Peloponnesian War.

be beneficial for the whole assemblage, both townsmen and foreigners, to heed them.

37 (1) We have a regime[10] that does not emulate the laws of our neighbors; rather than imitating others, we ourselves are a model for some. Because it is administered with a view not to the few but to the many, it has been called by the name "democracy." But while under the laws all receive equal treatment in private disputes, with regard to the question of merit, as each is well-reputed in some respect, so he is preferred in honor in our common affairs, not so much on the basis of lot as on the basis of virtue.[11] Nor is one who is poor but able to do some good for the city prevented from doing so by the obscurity of his position. (2) It is in a free manner that we govern our common affairs, and as for the suspicion of one another in everyday pursuits, we do not get angry at a neighbor if he does as he pleases; we do not even cast looks of reproach, which inflict no punishment but are distressing nonetheless. (3) Yet even though we are so unencumbered in our private associations, we are still, on account of fear above all, not lawless in our public conduct but obedient to whoever holds office and to the laws, especially those laws that are set down for the benefit of the victims of injustice and those unwritten laws that bring an avowed shame.

38 (1) Furthermore, we have provided the mind with the greatest relaxations from toils, making sanctioned use of games and sacrifices throughout the year, as well as of our elegant private buildings, the daily enjoyment of which drives out distress. (2) And

---

[10]  *Politeia,* which we translate here and at 36.4 as "regime," refers not only to the authoritative governing body and the arrangement of offices of the political association but also to its way of life and the end toward which it is directed.

[11]  There is some dispute among translators and commentators regarding whether *meros* refers to the "lot," the ancient practice of selecting representatives to the assembly, or to social standing based on class or family, or even more broadly to one's "allotted fate" (cf. Liddell, Scott, and Jones, *Greek-English Lexicon* [Oxford: Clarendon Press, 1992], *meros* IV.1; A.W. Gomme, *A Historical Commentary on Thucydides* [Oxford: Clarendon Press, 1966], p. 108; Simon Hornblower, *A Commentary on Thucydides,* volume 1 [Oxford: Clarendon Press, 1991], p. 300; J.S. Rusten, *Thucydides Book Two* [Cambridge: Cambridge University Press, 1989], pp. 144-145). Given the fact that Pericles' suggestion occurs in a statement that is a quiet qualification of the claim that Athens is a democracy, it is reasonable to infer that *meros* refers to the democratic lot. See Rusten's discussion of the contrasting *men - de* clauses and Hornblower's account of the various disagreements concerning Pericles' view of democracy.

due to our city's greatness, everything from every land is imported; hence, it is no more familiar to us to enjoy the goods produced here than to enjoy those produced by the rest of humanity.

39 (1) But we also differ from our opponents in military practices, in the following ways. We offer a city that is open to all, and never by the expulsion of foreigners do we prevent anyone from learning or seeing something which, if unconcealed, might benefit one of our enemies should he see it; we trust not so much in preparations and deceits as in the courage[12] that we bring to our tasks. In matters of education, whereas some seek after manliness through laborious training from early childhood, we do not live so austerely but no less advance to meet equal dangers.[13] (2) There is proof of this. For while the Lacedaemonians march into our land not by themselves[14] but with all their allies, we attack a neighboring land by ourselves, and even though we are fighting in a foreign place against those who are defending their homes, we usually prevail without difficulty. (3) And, in fact, no enemy has yet confronted our total power, because at the same time that we attend to our navy, we also dispatch our men on many land ventures. But if somewhere they tangle with some part of our power, they declare, when they prevail, that they repelled our entire force, and when they are conquered, that they were beaten by the same. (4) And yet if we are willing to face dangers more through easiness of temper than through laborious training and with a manliness not so much instilled by laws as arising from our ways, ours is the advantage, for we do not grow weary in the anticipation of hardships, and when we enter into them, we are manifestly no less daring than those who are forever laboring away. In these respects, our city is worthy of wonder, and in still others.

---

[12] Since the term *eupsuchia*, (lit., "goodness of soul") connotes courage, it has some overlap with the term *andreia* in the next sentence, which also means courage, and more precisely the courage of a man. In order to distinguish the two terms, we translate *eupsuchia* as "courage" and *andreia* as "manliness." Both terms are used again: *andreia* at 39.4 and *eupsuchia* at 43.4. Pericles will emphasize courage as a virtue of the Athenians also at 42.3 by speaking of the *andragathia*, "manly goodness," of those who died and at 42.2 by saying that the end these men have met demonstrates the *aretē andros*, "virtue of a man." See also Pericles' references to the "daring" (*tolma*) of the Athenians at 39.4, 40.3, 43.1, 41.4.

[13] Some commentators, e.g., Gomme, *A Historical Commentary on Thucydides*, pp. 117-8, understand the *isopaleis kindunoi*, "equal dangers," to mean dangers equal to Athenian capacity and not dangers equal to those that Athenian opponents encounter.

[14] Reading *heautous* with Valla.

40  (1) For we love beauty with economy, and we philosophize without softness.[15] Wealth we use as an opportunity for action rather than as a reason for boasting, and as for poverty, it is not shameful for someone to admit to it but surely so not to flee it by deed. (2) It is possible for those who care for the affairs of the city to care at the same time for their private affairs, and it is possible for the rest, those who go about their own business, to know the political things well enough. For we alone believe that one who has no share in these is not merely unpolitical[16] but useless. And indeed we ourselves at least judge policy correctly even if we are not personally the ones who draw it up, for we believe not that speeches are an impediment to deeds, but rather that the harm lies in not taking counsel in speech before going ahead with what must be done in deed. (3) In fact, we are so distinguished in this respect that in our endeavors we combine in the same persons both daring and calculation to the highest degree, whereas for others ignorance brings over-boldness and calculation brings hesitation. And those would justly be judged most superior in soul who know most clearly the terrible and pleasant things, and who do not as a result turn away from dangers. (4) So too, in what pertains to virtue, we have always been the opposite of most men. For we acquire friends not by being done a good turn but by doing one. The firmer friend is the one who has done a good turn, with the result that through his goodwill for the one he has helped, he preserves the gratitude owed; the less reliable friend is the one who is indebted, since he knows that it is not as a gracious gift but as a debt that he will repay his friend's virtue. (5) And we alone benefit another fearlessly, not so much through calculation of advantage as through trust in liberality.

41  (1) In sum, then, I say both that our whole city is the school of Greece and that, as individuals, each man from among us could, in my opinion, offer a body that is self-sufficient and capable of the most graceful versatility in the greatest number of roles. (2) The very power of our city, which we have acquired as a result of the ways I have spoken of, is a sign that these things are

---

[15]  Pericles uses two parallel verbs here: *philokalēnai* and *philosophēnai*. The first verb, which we translate as " love beauty" could also be translated as "love the noble."

[16]  The Greek term *apragmona*, which we translate as "unpolitical," is generally used as a term of praise: it means "not to be a meddler," or "to mind one's own business." See Gomme, *A Historical Commentary on Thucydides*, pp. 121-122.

not a boast in speech for the sake of the present occasion but, rather, that they are true to the actual deeds. (3) For our city alone of the current powers proves when tested to be superior to what is said of her, and she alone gives no grounds either for her attackers to be vexed about the sort of people by whom they have been harmed, or for her subjects to complain that they are being ruled by those who are unworthy. (4) Leaving great monuments and securing a power that is certainly not without witness, we shall be marveled at by our contemporaries as well as by future generations, and we have no need in addition of praise from a Homer or from anyone else whose verses may please for the moment but will have their intended effect harmed by the truth of the actual deeds. Instead, we have compelled every sea and land to become a pathway for our daring, and have everywhere established everlasting memorials of deeds bad and good. (5) It was for such a city, because they thought it just not to be deprived of her, that these men here nobly fought and died. And it is fitting for everyone left behind to be willing to suffer on her behalf.

42  (1) Indeed, this is why I have dwelt upon what pertains to our city, to teach you that what is at stake for us in our struggle is not equivalent to what is at stake for others for whom there is nothing comparable, and at the same time to clarify with specifics the eulogy of those over whom I am now speaking. (2) The greatest part of my eulogy has already been delivered. For the qualities for which I have sung the city's praise have been adorned by the virtues of these men and those like them. Not many of the Greeks could match their deeds to this account, as these men have. The end that these men have now met, it seems to me, demonstrates the virtue of a man, either in its first flower or in its final confirmation. (3) And even for those who were rather bad in other respects, it is just that preference be given to their manly goodness in wars fought on behalf of the fatherland. For wiping out bad with good, they have done more public-spirited benefit than they did privately-motivated harm. (4) Of these men, none was made soft by preferring the continued enjoyment of his wealth, nor did any shrink from the danger in the hope that attends poverty, that one might yet flee it and become wealthy. Holding vengeance against their enemies to be more desirable than these things, and at the same time believing this to be the noblest of risks, they chose, accordingly, to seek vengeance and simply to long for[17]

---

[17]  Reading *ephiesthai*, "to long for," with the mss. instead of *aphiesthai*, "to let go of," with Poppo. Since the reading of the manuscripts is perfectly plau-

the other things. Consigning to hope the uncertainty of their future prosperity, they thought it fit to entrust themselves with the task then before them. And in this task, believing it better to fight and to suffer than to save themselves by capitulating, they fled the shame that would come in speech, and with their bodies they stood firm at their task. And, in the chance of a moment, with their fame rather than their fear at its peak, they were set free.

43 (1) These men, then, were of such a character as befits our city. Those who remain ought to pray to have a resolve in the face of the enemy that is less perilous but also to deem it worthy to have one that is no less daring. Do not consider by reason alone the benefit, which someone, by saying all the good things that come from repelling the enemy, could lay out before you who know it just as well; but rather as a daily deed contemplate the power of our city and become lovers of her.[18] And when she seems to you to be great, reflect that men have acquired all this through daring, through knowledge of what was needed, and through a sense of shame amidst their actions, and that whenever they failed in one of their attempts, they did not think it worthy to deprive the city of their virtue, but they bestowed upon her the noblest contribution. (2) Giving their bodies in common, individually they received an ageless praise and a burial place of the greatest distinction, not so much where each lies as where his fame is laid up, ever to be remembered on occasions that present an opportunity for speech or deed. (3) For illustrious men the whole earth is

sible, there does not seem to be warrant for the emendation. The longing for the other things does not cease, as *aphiesthai* would imply; indeed, the soldiers' choice to seek vengeance in the face of this longing is more impressive than if they should have ceased to have had any concern at all for these other objects. Cf. Gomme, *A Historical Commentary on Thucydides*, p. 132; Rusten, *Thucydides Book Two*, p. 166.

[18]   It is possible for the genitive *autēs*, "of her," to refer to either of the two feminine nouns in the sentence: city (*polis*) or power (*dunamis*). Thus, Pericles might be urging the Athenians to become lovers of the power of Athens, not of Athens herself. His next observation could reasonably be understood also to refer to the power of the city as opposed to the city itself: "And when [it] seems to you to be great...". Since, however, the full context of the Pericles' exhortation is a praise of the city, and he goes on to say that the listeners should reflect upon the fact that "whenever [the soldiers] failed in one of their attempts, they did not think it worthy to deprive the city of their virtue, but they handed her the noblest contribution," it seems more plausible that he is urging the listeners to become lovers of Athens herself.

a burial place, and not only do the burial markers at home commemorate them but even abroad there lives for each an unwritten memorial, resting more in the minds of men than in any physical marker. (4) You here now, emulate these men and judge happiness to be freedom, and freedom to be courage, and do not pause before the dangers of war. (5) For it is not those who fare ill who would with greater justice be extravagant with their lives, those who have no hope of anything good, but those who, in living, still risk a turn for the worse and who have the most to lose should they stumble in some way. (6) Indeed, the degradation that accompanies softness is more grievous to a man of pride than is the unfelt death that comes to pass amidst strength and a shared hope.

44   (1) Thus, I do not lament for the parents of these men, all those of you that are here now, but rather I offer encouragement. For the parents know that they reared their sons amidst the many turns of circumstance. Fortunate are those who have received as their fate that which is most becoming—as have these in their end, and you in your grief—and for whom life ends at a point commensurate with the happiness in which it was lived. (2) Now, I know that it is difficult to persuade you of this, since you will often find, in the good fortune of others, reminders of the good fortune in which you too once delighted. There is no pain when one is deprived of goods he has not experienced but only when he is stripped of that to which he has become accustomed. (3) You must take strength in the hope of other children to come, you who are still of the age to have them. For those children who are yet to be born will help some of you individually forget the ones who are no more, and for the city, they will bring a double benefit by making it both less deserted and safer. And indeed it is impossible for those who do not take a risk, by equally putting their children too at stake, to deliberate at all equally or justly. (4) As for you who are past that age, believe that the greater part of your life, during which you were fortunate, was a gain, and that the rest will be brief, and be heartened by the renown of these men. For only the love of honor is ageless, and it is not gaining profit, as some say, but being honored that brings delight to those who are past the age at which they were useful.

45   (1) As for you children and brothers of these men, I see that your struggle is formidable, since all are wont to praise the one who is no more, and even though you may prove to be of surpassing virtue, scarcely will you be judged equal but rather a little inferior. For the living incur envy because they are to be competed

with, whereas the one who is no impediment is honored with a goodwill free of antagonism. (2) But if I must also make some mention of the feminine virtue to those who will now be widows, I shall put it all in a brief piece of advice: your reputation will be great if you do not become inferior to your proper nature, as will the reputation of she who is spoken of least among the men, either in praise of her virtue or in reproach.

46 (1) And so I, too, in accordance with the law, have put forth in speech all that I had to say that is fitting. As for deeds, while those being buried have already been adorned in some respects, in addition the city will henceforth rear their children at the public expense until they reach maturity, providing this benefit to these men and those they leave behind as a crowning wreath for their struggles. For where the greatest prizes for virtue have been set down, there the best men will engage in politics.[19] (2) Now that you have lamented those whom it is fitting for each of you to lament, depart.

---

[19]    An alternative translation is given by Rusten, *Thucydides Book Two*, p. 178: "those who establish the greatest rewards for virtue, possess the best citizens."

# PLATO'S MENEXENUS

234a   *Socrates.* From the agora[1] or from where, Menexenus?[2]

*Menexenus.* From the agora, Socrates, and from the council-chamber.

*Socrates.* What in particular drew you to the council-chamber? Or is it clear that you believe you have come to the end of education and philosophy, and, supposing yourself sufficiently prepared, you intend to turn to greater things? Will you try at such a young age, wondrous one, to rule us, your elders, so that your house will never cease to provide us with a caretaker?

*Menexenus.* If you, Socrates, permit and advise me to rule, I'll be eager; but if not, I won't. In this instance, however, I went to the council-chamber since I had learned that the Council was about to choose the one who will speak over those who have died. For you know that they intend to hold a funeral.

*Socrates.* Certainly. But whom did they choose?

---

[1]   The *agora* was the civic center of Athens, situated between the Acropolis and the main city gate. Countless examples in ancient Greek literature attest to its importance to community life in Athens. The council-chamber (*boulesterion*), mentioned in the next line, was where the council of Athens met daily to perform the deliberative, administrative, and judicial functions of government necessary for implementing the policies of the assembly.

[2]   It is clear from this dialogue alone that Socrates and Menexenus are friends. But Menexenus is also named in the *Phaedo* (59b) among those companions who attended Socrates at his death. In a younger incarnation, he is one of the two main interlocutors in the *Lysis*, Plato's dialogue on friendship. Even at his young age in the *Lysis*, he appears to be acquainted with Socrates, perhaps through his cousin Ctesippus (207a-b). In the *Menexenus* itself, Menexenus must be around the age of eighteen since he is represented as about to take up the political duties and privileges of an Athenian citizen.

33

*Menexenus.* No one. They put it off until tomorrow. I expect, though, that Archinus or Dion will be chosen.[3]

c     *Socrates.* Indeed, Menexenus, dying in war seems in many ways to be noble.[4] For even if the one who has died[5] was poor, he receives a fine and magnificent funeral, and even if he was worthless, he receives praise from wise men who do not praise at random but prepare speeches long beforehand. These men praise so beautifully that by giving each man qualities he actually possessed and even some he didn't, going to every length to most beauti-

235a     fully embellish with their words, they bewitch our souls. They pay every manner of tribute to the city, to those who have died in war, and to all our earlier ancestors. And they even praise us, the living, such that I for my part, Menexenus, feel altogether elevated

b     by their praises.[6] Each time, as I listen and am charmed, I am altered, believing that I've become at that moment greater, more dignified, and more beautiful. Often some foreigners follow along and listen with me, and in their eyes too I become instantly more majestic. And indeed, it seems to me that they, having been seduced by the speaker, feel the same things towards the rest of the

---

3     Archinus was an important political figure during the re-establishment of democracy in Athens in 403 B.C. There are three political actions for which he is chiefly remembered. He intentionally prevented the oligarchs from emigrating to Eleusis (a haven for disaffected oligarchs); he vehemently and successfully resisted Thrasybulus' suggestion that Athenian citizenship be extended to all those who contributed to the re-establishment of democracy; and he sentenced to death the first man who violated the amnesty guaranteed to those who were involved in the oligarchy. See John V. A. Fine, *The Ancient Greeks: A Critical History* (Cambridge, MA: Belknap Press, 1983), pp. 523-525; George Grote, *History of Greece*, vol. 8, (New York: Harper Brothers, 1855) pp. 267-276. Dion the Athenian is mentioned by Xenophon as one of the Athenian ambassadors sent in an unsuccessful attempt to negotiate with the Persians in 392 B.C. (*Hellenica* IV.7.13).

4     On *kalos*, "noble," see note 2 to preceding translation of Pericles' Funeral Oration. In this translation, we generally render *kalos* as "noble," with a few exceptions when we use "beautiful" or "fine."

5     The Greek verb *apothneiskein* means simply "to die off." It does not carry the same range of meaning, nor the gentle euphemism, of *teleutan* which means "to bring to an end" in the sense of completion, accomplishment, or fulfillment. This use of *apothneiskein* is more the exception than the rule in Socrates' speech. *Apothneiskein* is used only at 234b and 234c; *teleutan* and related terms, by contrast, are used at 234c, 235a, 236d, 236e, 237a, 238c, 242e, 244a, 246a, 246d, 248b, c, d, e, 249b and c.

6     We translate here the adverbial form of the Greek term *gennaios*, which most precisely means "nobly born," as "elevated" and its comparative in the next sentence as "more dignified," in order to distinguish it from the instances of *kalos*.

c    city as they feel towards me, believing her to be more wondrous than before. This sense of majesty stays with me for more than three days. The speech is so fresh and the speaker's voice so rings in my ears that scarcely on the fourth or fifth day do I remember who I am and notice that I am of this earth—in the meantime I almost believe that I live on the Isles of the Blessed.[7] Such is the cleverness of our rhetoricians.

*Menexenus.* You are always making fun of the rhetoricians, Socrates. In this instance, to be sure, I expect that the one they choose won't do so well, for the whole selection has arisen on the spur of the moment so that the speaker may well be forced to speak virtually off-hand.

d    *Socrates.* How so, good fellow? Each of them have speeches already prepared, and in any event it is not hard to speak off-hand in such situations. Now, if one should have to speak well of Athenians before Peloponnesians, or of Peloponnesians before Athenians, then one would have to be a good rhetorician to persuade and win esteem. But when someone competes before the very ones he is praising, it is no great thing to seem to speak well.

e    *Menexenus.* You don't think so, Socrates?

*Socrates.* Certainly not, by Zeus.

*Menexenus.* Do you think that you yourself would be able to speak, if you should have to and the Council should choose you?

*Socrates.* That I would be able to speak, Menexenus, is nothing wondrous. For I happen to have a teacher who is not at all bad in rhetoric, but who has produced, in addition to many other great rhetoricians, the one who is preeminent among the Greeks— Pericles, son of Xanthippus.

*Menexenus.* Who is this teacher? Or is it clear that you mean Aspasia?[8]

---

[7]    The "Isles of the Blessed" are mentioned twice in Book Seven of Plato's *Republic* (519c, 540b).

[8]    Aspasia was best known as a courtesan, and as a result of her infamous relation with Pericles, she was often blamed by the comedians for interfering in Athens' political affairs (see especially Aristophanes' *Acharnians* 523-532). In his life of Pericles, Plutarch indicates that the reference to Aspasia in the *Menexenus* is a joke, but he observes that we may take as true the claim that Aspasia had much skill in the art of speaking, so much so that several Athenians came to her for instruction (Plutarch, *Lives*, translated by John Dryden [New York: Modern Library, 1932], p. 200); See also Louis Méridier, ed. *Platon Oeuvres Complètes*, tome 5 (Paris: Les Belles Lettres, 1931) pp. 78-79, Paul Friedländer, *Plato II: The Dialogues*, translated by Hans Meyerhoff (London: Routledge & Kegan Paul, 1964) pp. 219-220.

*Socrates.* Yes, her, and Connus, son of Metrobius. These two are
236a    my teachers, he of music, and she of rhetoric. So it is nothing
wondrous that a man trained in this way should be clever at speaking. Even someone who has been educated worse than I—in music
by Lamprus, in rhetoric by Antiphon of Rhamnusia[9]—could still
win esteem when praising Athenians before Athenians.

*Menexenus.* And what would you have to say, if you should have
to speak?

*Socrates.* Of my own, perhaps nothing. But just yesterday I heard
b     Aspasia going through a funeral speech for these same dead. For
she had heard what you mention, that the Athenians were about
to choose the one who will speak. So she narrated for me the sort
of things that ought to be said; some of these she came up with
on the spur of the moment, and others she had previously prepared by gluing together leftovers from the time when, I believe,
she was composing the funeral speech Pericles delivered.

*Menexenus.* And can you remember what Aspasia said?

*Socrates.* I'd be unjust if I couldn't. After all, I learned it from her,
c     and I almost caught a beating whenever I forgot something.

*Menexenus.* Why don't you narrate it now then?

*Socrates.* But I fear that my teacher will be angry with me if I divulge
her speech.

*Menexenus.* Never mind that, Socrates, just speak and you will
gratify me greatly. Whether you wish to give Aspasia's speech or
whomever's, just speak.

*Socrates.* But perhaps you'll laugh at me if in my old age I seem
to you still to be playing.

*Menexenus.* Not at all, Socrates. But by all means, speak.

---

9     Antiphon was a famous Attic rhetorician and teacher of rhetoric. A book
of oratorical exercises, the *Tetralogies*, is accredited to him and is considered the foundation for the genre of Attic rhetoric (Hammond, *A History
of Greece to 322 B.C.,* 3rd ed., [Oxford: Clarendon Press, 1986], p. 432). He
was the intellectual leader of the oligarchic conspiracy in 411 B.C., and
was tried and executed after the fall of the Four Hundred (Hammond, *A
History of Greece,* p. 406; Grote, *History of Greece,* vol. 6, pp. 15-17, 26-38, 74-
77). The only public speech he is known to have given was at his own
trial. Thucydides records that it was the finest speech of its kind ever heard
(Thucydides VIII.68), but it was unsuccessful nonetheless. Lamprus, ac-
cording to Athenaeus, was Sophocles' instructor in music and dance
(*Deinosophists* 20f). By his contemporary, the tragic poet Phrynicus,
Lamprus was considered to be a charlatan (*Deinosophists* 44d; C.E. Graves,
*The "Euthyphro" and "Menexenus" of Plato,* (London: Macmillan and Co.,
Limited, 1935) p. 91.

*Socrates.* Well, I guess I must gratify you, seeing as how, since we
d    are alone, I'd very nearly gratify you even if you were to urge me
to dance naked. But listen. For starting with the ones who themselves had died, she spoke, I believe, as follows:

With respect to deeds, these men have received from us what
befits them, for they depart on the destined journey having been
sent forth as a group by the city and individually by their families. But as for speech, the law enjoins us to give these men the
e    honor still due, and it is proper that we do so. For when deeds
have been well performed, a finely delivered speech can instill in
the listeners remembrance and honor for those who have done
the deeds. Such a speech must adequately praise those who have
died and graciously counsel those who are living, urging children and brothers to imitate the virtue of the ones who lie before
them, and consoling fathers, mothers, and any other surviving
237a    ancestors. How can we find such a speech? Where would we
rightly begin to praise good men, who in life pleased those around
them by their virtue and who died in exchange for the safety of
the living? It seems to me that as they were good, one ought naturally to praise them as such. But they were good because they
grew from the good. Let us pay tribute first, then, to their good
b    birth, and, second, to their nurture and education; after this, let
us describe the performance of their deeds, how noble and worthy a display they made of them.

To begin with, the basis of their good birth is that their ancestors
were not born in a foreign land, and thus they, the descendants,
did not migrate to this country, with ancestors from elsewhere.
No, they were autochthonous, living and dwelling in their true
fatherland, nurtured not by a stepmother as others are but by a
mother, the country in which they lived. And now in death, they
c    lie in their familial places in the country that bore, nurtured, and
has received them back again. It is therefore most just to honor
first their mother herself, as this will be to honor at the same time
the goodness of their birth.

Our country is worthy of praise not only from us but from all
mankind. There are many reasons for this, but the first and greatest is that she happens to be loved by the gods. Witness to our
claim is the strife and quarrel of the gods who disputed over her.[10]

---

[10]    According to legend, Poseidon and Athena contended over the posses-
sion of Athens. Each gave the Athenians a gift: Poseidon, a well of sea-

d     She whom gods praised, how could it not be just that she be praised by all of humanity?

Second, it is just that she be praised because in the time when the whole earth was producing and begetting the many animals, wild and tame, our own land proved to be pure, barren of the wild and savage; from among the animals, she chose for herself and bore man, who surpasses the rest in understanding and alone

e     recognizes justice and the gods. There is great proof for this claim that our land bore our ancestors, the ancestors we share with the men now lying before us. For each thing that bears has the ap-

238a    propriate nourishment for that which it bears, and by this it is clear whether a woman has truly given birth. If she has not, but has substituted a child in place of having her own, she lacks sources of nourishment for the child. And indeed, our own land, our mother, provides adequate proof that she brought forth human beings. For in that time she alone first brought forth human nourishment, the fruit of wheat and barley, by which the human race is most finely and excellently nourished, since this in fact was the animal she bore. It is more fitting, too, to accept such a proof on behalf of the land than on behalf of a woman, for the land has not imitated woman in pregnancy and birth, but woman, land. And she did not horde these fruits but distributed them to others as well.[11] After this, she brought forth for her descendants the olive, a balm for the pains of labor. And having nurtured and

b     raised her descendants to manhood, she led forth the gods to be their rulers and teachers—the names of whom it is fitting to leave out in this instance, since we know them—and they equipped us to live, securing our daily existence by educating us in the basic arts, and preparing us to guard our country by teaching us the acquisition and use of weapons.

Having thus been born and educated, the ancestors of the men lying here lived in a regime they established, which it is correct

c     to recall briefly. For it is the regime that nurtures human beings, a noble regime, good ones, the opposite, bad ones. Thus it is necessary to show that those who came before us were nurtured in a noble regime, on account of which they were good, as are men

---

water; Athena, an olive tree. Zeus intervened to prevent the contest from becoming violent, and a divine court voted by a margin of one that Athena had given the better gift and that she should have Athens (Graves, *The "Euthyphro" and "Menexenus" of Plato*, p. 95; Herodotus VIII.55).

[11]    Compare Thucydides' more negative description of the original condition of the Attic land (I.2).

now, including these who have died. After all, the same regime existed then as now—an aristocracy, in which at present we live as citizens, as we have almost continually since then. Although one man calls her a democracy, another something else that pleases

d   him, in truth she is an aristocracy with the approval of the multitude. For we have always had kings, sometimes by birth, at other times chosen.[12] And although the multitude has control over most of the city's affairs, they give the ruling offices and authority to those who are consistently deemed to be best; and, unlike what happens in other cities, no one has ever been left out because of weakness or poverty or the obscurity of his father, nor has anyone ever been honored for the opposites. Rather, there is one standard: he who is deemed to be wise or good has authority and

e   rules. The cause of this, our regime, is its origin in equality. For the other cities have been constructed from all sorts of unequal human beings, with the result that their regimes—tyrannies and oligarchies—are also unequal. They live, therefore, regarding

239a  some as slaves and others as masters. But since we and our people have all grown as brothers of one mother, we do not think it right to be slaves or masters of one another. Instead, our equality of birth, our natural equality, makes it necessary to seek equality under law, legal equality, and to yield to one another for no reason other than reputation for virtue and prudence.

It is because of this that the fathers of these men here and our fathers and these men themselves, having been raised in complete freedom and having grown up nobly, proved themselves before all human beings in many noble deeds, private and pub-

b   lic. They performed these deeds out of the belief that it is necessary on behalf of freedom to fight both Greeks on behalf of other Greeks, and Barbarians on behalf of all the Greeks. How they defended themselves when Eumolpus and the Amazons and those still earlier were invading our country, and how they defended the Argives against the Cadmeians, and the Heracleidae against the Argives, our time is too brief to give the narration

[12]   Socrates' remark here is not inaccurate, but it may be misleading. The power of the Athenian kingship had been severely limited since late in the eighth century. And it is likely that approximately 682 B.C. marked the final end of the hereditary kingship in Athens; at that time the position became an annual magistracy, reserved for presiding over religious matters. The position, however, retained the title *basileus* (king). (See Aristotle, *Constitution of Athens* 8; *Politics* 1273b-1274a; Fine, *The Ancient Greeks*, pp. 181-182; Graves, *The "Euthyphro" and "Menexenus" of Plato*, p. 97).

deserved.[13] And besides, by having already beautifully sung of their virtue in music, the poets have made it known to all. If we

c     were to try to honor the same deeds in bare speech, we would probably appear second-best. So, for these reasons, I think it best to pass over these deeds, considering also that they have received their due. But concerning those for which no poet has yet a worthy reputation for capturing their worth, those deeds which remain forgotten, I think we ought to recall them to memory by praising them and by encouraging others to set them down in odes and other poetry as befits the men who performed them. These are the deeds I shall speak of first.

d     When the Persians were dominating Asia and attempting to enslave Europe, they encountered the descendants of this country, our progenitors whom it is just and fitting to remember first and to praise for their virtue. Now, in order to praise it finely, one must cast oneself back in thought to that time when all of Asia was already enslaved by the third King. The first of the Kings, Cyrus, freed his own countrymen, the Persians, and at the same time en-

e     slaved to his own will their masters, the Medes, and he became ruler of the rest of Asia as far as Egypt. His son then added Egypt and Libya, as much of them as he was able to traverse. The third, Darius, by foot extended the empire's boundary all the way to Scythia, and by ships controlled the sea and the islands. As a re-

240a     sult, no one even deemed himself a rival to him, and the minds of all human beings were enslaved. This is how the Persian empire reduced many great and warlike races to slavery.[14]

---

[13]     Socrates is speaking here of the legendary pre-history of Athens. The Greeks traditionally understood the Dorian invasions of the early second millennium B.C. as the return of the sons of Heracles (the Heracleidae) who were banished from Mycenae. According to legend, they returned to take their former homeland in the Peloponnesus with the help of the Athenians (Fine, *The Ancient Greeks*, p. 16; Grote, *History of Greece*, vol. 1, pp. 84-85). The war with the Eleusinian king, Eumolpus, along with the Amazon invasion and the "defense" of the Argives, are the events surrounding Theseus' famous *synoecism*—his unification of the cities in Attica which took place in roughly the thirteenth century B.C. (Thucydides II.15; Graves, *The "Euthyphro" and "Menexenus" of Plato*, p. 98; Fine, *The Ancient Greeks*, p. 178).

[14]     Socrates refers in this paragraph to the expansion of the Persian empire that took place under Cyrus the Great (550-530 B.C.), Cambyses (530-522 B.C.), and Darius I (522-485). For aiding the revolt of the Ionians in 499 B.C.—during which the Persians subjugated the Greek cities in Ionia, taking Miletus in 494 along with the islands of Chios, Lesbos, and Tenedos—Athens and Eretria were marked for punishment by Darius. Following the invasion of Thrace in 492, which extended Persian control to the north-

Then Darius, accusing us and the Eretrians, on the pretext that we were plotting against Sardis, sent 500,000 men on transports and 300 war ships, and he told Datis, the commander, to return with Eretrians and Athenians in tow, if he should wish to keep

b    his head. Sailing to Eretria against men who were among the most esteemed warriors of the Greeks of that time and who were not few in number, Datis subdued them in three days. In order that no one might escape, he searched through their entire country in the following manner: his soldiers, going to the Eretrian borders,

c    spread out from sea to sea, joined hands, and went through the entire country so that they could say to the King that no one had eluded them.[15] With the same intention, they went down from Eretria to Marathon, believing themselves ready to yoke the Athenians with the Eretrians under this same necessity. When the former deeds were being done, and the latter being attempted, none of the Greeks came to the aid of either the Eretrians or the Athenians—except the Spartans, and they arrived the day after

d    the battle; all the rest were panic-stricken and, embracing their present safety, kept quiet. Anyone who looks back to that time, then, would know what sort of men they were in virtue, they who met the power of the Barbarians at Marathon and punished the arrogance of all of Asia. The first to raise trophies over the Barbarians, they became leaders and teachers to others that the power of the Persians was not invincible but that any multitude

e    of men and all wealth yields to virtue. And so I say that these men are fathers not only of our bodies but also of our freedom, ours and that of everyone on this continent. For looking to this deed even in later battles, the Greeks dared to run every risk in defense of their safety, having become students of those at Marathon.[16]

ern border of Thessaly, Darius set his sights on the mainland Greeks who had aided the Ionian revolt. See Grote, *History of Greece*, vol. 4, pp. 349-435 and vol. 5, pp. 1-86, for a full history of this long period.

[15]    Eretria was besieged by the Persians in 490 B.C. The six-day siege ended when the city was betrayed from within. The Athenians sent military aid, but they were told upon their arrival that the situation was hopeless and that they should return to Athens. Herodotus records that all of the inhabitants were taken captive back to Persia (Herodotus VI.100-101). Herodotus does not mention the tactics described here, but Plato offers a similar account in the *Laws* 698c-699c (see also Graves, *The "Euthyphro" and "Menexenus" of Plato*, p. 101; Grote, *History of Greece*, vol. 5, pp. 43-47).

[16]    In the famous battle of Marathon a vastly outnumbered Athenian army successfully repelled an invading Persian force. According to Herodotus, the battle was extraordinarily one-sided; 6,400 Persians were killed, compared to only 192 Athenians (Herodotus VI.102-120). Socrates does not

Thus, to the men who fought at Marathon, we must give the highest prize in our speech. But the second place must go to those
241a     who fought and won the sea-battles around Salamis and at
Artemisium.[17] About these men too, one would have many things to tell, both the kind of attacks they endured by land and by sea, and the way they fought off these attacks. But I shall recall to your memory what seems to me to have been the noblest of their deeds, since it advanced the work begun by those at Marathon. For those at Marathon proved to the Greeks only so much: that
b        on land it was possible to fight off the Barbarians, even with few against many. But it was still unclear on the sea, where the Persians had the reputation of being invincible due to their numbers, wealth, skill, and strength. So this is why it is fitting to praise the men who fought the sea-battles at that time, because they dispelled the Greeks' second fear, relieving them of the fright inspired by a great number of ships and men. Hence, it came about
c        that by both those who fought at Marathon and those who fought the sea-battles at Salamis, the rest of the Greeks were educated, learning from the former the lesson on land, from the latter the lesson at sea; they were trained not to fear the Barbarians.

Third, I declare, third both in order and in virtue in securing the safety of Greece, is the deed at Plataea, a common venture now

---

mention the indirect but important influence of the Spartans on the battle. Although they were not present at the battle, the news that they were committing troops to the endeavor significantly raised the morale of the Athenians and induced the Persians to make the hasty and, ultimately illadvised, strategic decision to divide their forces (Grote, *History of Greece*, vol. 5, pp. 47-73).

[17]   In the naval battle of Salamis (480 B.C.), an allied Greek fleet (roughly half Athenian) engaged and defeated a Persian fleet in the strait between Salamis and mainland Greece. Herodotus attributes the victory largely to the wiles of Themistocles, who incited the engagement by sending a messenger to the Persians with false reports of strife within the Greek fleet (Herodotus VIII.56-96; Fine, *The Ancient Greeks*, pp. 312-314; Grote, *History of Greece*, vol. 5, 228-252). Not much is known about the details of the naval engagement at Artemisium that took place contemporaneously with the battle of Thermopylae. What is known is that an allied Greek fleet won a pyrrhic victory there against the Persian fleet (Herodotus VIII. 7-14, 18; Fine, *The Ancient Greeks*, pp. 303-4; Grote, *History of Greece*, vol. 5, pp. 208-215). We know from Thucydides (III.54) that Athenians and Spartans fought side by side in this engagement, although Socrates does not mention this.

of Spartans and Athenians.[18] In fact, the threat all these men fought off was the greatest and most difficult, and for their virtue they are praised now by us, as they will be by future generations.

d   But after this, many Greek cities were still siding with the Barbarian, and the King himself was reported to be planning another attack on the Greeks. It is just, then, that we recall also those who brought their predecessors' deeds to their conclusion of full safety by clearing away the whole Barbarian force and driving it off the sea. These were the men who fought the sea-battle at the

e   Eurymedon, who marched at Cyprus, and who sailed to Egypt and many other places.[19] It is right to remember and be grateful to them, for they frightened the King into turning his mind towards his own safety and away from plotting the destruction of the Greeks.

---

[18]   A crucial victory over the Persian army was won at Plataea (479 B.C.). Socrates finally has mentioned the contribution of the Spartans to the defense of Greece. By all accounts Spartan valor contributed decisively to the victory. The Greeks showed no mercy to the defeated army; taking no prisoners, the Greeks slaughtered the Persian army to the last man. Only a small group escaped by land to Asia Minor (Herodotus IX.31-70; Fine, *The Ancient Greeks,* pp. 319-320). It is not clear whether the Spartans were principally responsible for the slaughter that ensued after the battle was decided (Grote, *History of Greece,* vol. 5, pp. 279-291).

[19]   Socrates is actually describing the events surrounding the Athenian expansion. The campaigns Socrates recounts (Eurymedon 469 B.C., Cyprus, and Egypt 459-454 B.C.) were conducted as much to justify the use of Delian League funds for the Athenian navy as out of fear of the Persians. The Delian League was initially formed by a group of Aegean islands led by Athens and guided by the common purpose of waging war on Persia, an endeavor of which the Spartans wanted no part (Thucydides I.96; Fine, 332). This was the beginning of the rift between the Spartan-led Hellenic League and the Athenian-led Delian League. The members of the Delian League were required to provide a given number of ships annually to the collective fleet. With increasing frequency, cash payments were made to Athens in lieu of providing ships and crews. The Athenians encouraged the policy of cash payments, and by the 440's only Lesbos, Chios, and Samos were providing their own ships. All the other members of the Delian League were in effect paying Athens for protection. At Eurymedon (469 B.C.) the Athenians fought and defeated a large force of Persians who were allegedly preparing to raid the Greek cities of the Ionian coast (Thucydides I.100; Fine, *The Ancient Greeks,* p. 344; Grote, *History of Greece,* vol. 5, pp. 395-397). The Athenians moved into Cyprus, and from there to Egypt (Thucydides I.94, 104, 110, 112; Grote, *The Ancient Greeks,* vol. 5, pp. 408-419). The Egyptian campaign was a complete and costly failure. Thucydides writes of it : "Thus, the efforts of the Greeks came to nothing after six years of war" (Thucydides I.110).

242a This war against the Barbarians was endured by our whole city, on our own behalf as well as on behalf of the rest who speak the same language. But when peace came and our city was honored, she became the object of that which human beings are prone to feel towards those who are successful: first emulation, and then, from emulation, envy. This pushed our city unwillingly into war with the Greeks.

b After this war began, we engaged the Spartans at Tanagra fighting on behalf of Boeotian freedom.[20] And though the outcome of the battle was disputed, the subsequent deed decided it. For while the Spartans departed and left behind those whom they had come to aid, our own men, winning a victory on the third day in Oenophyta, justly restored those who had been unjustly banished. Now helping Greeks against Greeks on behalf of freedom, these were the first after the Persian war to become good men[21] and to free those whom they were helping. Honored by the city, they were the first to be laid to rest in this monument.

c

Later, once a larger war had broken out and all the Greeks had attacked and ravaged our country, repaying our city with such unworthy thanks, our men vanquished them in a sea-battle and seized their Spartan leaders at Sphacteria. Having it then in their power to destroy them, they nevertheless spared and returned d them, and made peace.[22] They believed that whereas they ought

[20] In the battle of Tanagra (457 B.C.), an army of Spartans, after completing a mission to quell Phocian hostilities, feared that the Athenians would attack them if they returned home across the Gulf of Corinth or through Megara, because both were guarded by the Athenians. A faction of Athenian oligarchs encouraged them to camp at Tanagra, which they did. The democratic Athenians, perceiving this as a threat, sent out a force which engaged and was defeated by the Spartans and their allies. Sixty-two days later, after the Spartans had fled for the Peloponnese, the Athenians attacked Tanagra, destroyed its fortifications, and took as hostages one hundred of the wealthiest people in the region. In Thucydides' account, the event seems far more like conquest than "liberation" (Thucydides I.108; Grote, *History of Greece*, vol. 5, pp. 413-414; Fine, *The Ancient Greeks*, p. 354-5).

[21] See note 3 to our translation of Pericles' Funeral Oration.

[22] Socrates is speaking of an event that took place seven years into the Peloponnesian War. Sphacteria is an island near Pylos, where the Athenians decisively defeated a Peloponnesian fleet (425 B.C). This victory left the Spartans in the embarrassing situation of having an army stranded on the small island of Sphacteria and brought them to plead for an armistice. After a remarkable victory by Demosthenes and Cleon against the Spartan garrison on the island, the Spartans survivors surrendered and were brought to Athens (Thucydides IV.1-39; Grote, *History of Greece*, vol. 6, pp. 326-362; Fine,*The Ancient Greeks*, pp. 478-80). Up to this point, the war had

to wage war against the Barbarians all the way to destruction, they should fight those of their own race only to the point of victory, and should not let the anger of a single city destroy the community of the Greeks. It is certainly fitting to praise the men who fought in that war and lie here, because though some might try to claim that in the earlier war against the Barbarians there were others better than the Athenians, these men proved that this could

e    not be true. For this time, prevailing in war in a Greece divided by rebellion and subduing the foremost of the other Greeks, they proved victorious on their own over those with whom they had once united to conquer the Barbarian.

After this peace came a third war, unexpected and terrible, in which many good men who now lie here died. Many of them sailed to regions around Sicily where they raised a great number

243a    of trophies on behalf of the freedom of the Leontinians, whom they were helping in keeping with their oaths.[23] But when the length of their voyage became a problem for our city and left her unable to aid them, they gave up and fell into misfortune—these men of whom the very enemies that fought them received more praise for moderation and virtue than do the friends of other

---

not been going well for the Athenians. Encouraged by their new success, they were impassive toward Spartan pleas for peace until they themselves met with defeat at Delium and Amphipolis. Only at that time were they willing to make a treaty involving the lifting of the siege on Sphacteria (Thucydides IV.1-39, V.14; Fine, *The Ancient Greeks*, pp. 478-80).

[23]    In June of 415, the Athenians launched their famous and ill-fated campaign against Sicily, on the pretext of aiding certain Sicilian cities against others. Socrates speaks of this campaign as if it was distinct from the war with the Spartans, but by all accounts it was an almost seamless continuation of the Peloponnesian War. The expedition was plagued by problems of leadership. The Athenians sent three generals to Sicily: Lamachus, Alcibiades, and Nicias. Lamachus was killed in battle. As a result of agitation by his political enemies, Alcibiades was called back to Athens to stand trial for impiety. Perceiving that conditions in Athens at that time were highly unfavorable to him and that such a trial would surely mean his demise, Alcibiades fled to Sparta, where he treacherously informed the Spartans of the Athenians' designs in Sicily and strongly encouraged them to send military aid to Syracuse. These developments left in charge of the army only Nicias, who had had strong misgivings about the expedition at its inception and had joined it reluctantly. Demosthenes joined Nicias in the summer of 413, but the expedition came to a disastrous end in September when 40,000 Athenians surrendered to the Syracusians, who slaughtered thousands on the spot and worked the rest to death as quarry slaves (Thucydides Books VI-VII; Fine, *The Ancient Greeks*, pp. 491-97; Grote, *History of Greece*, vol. 6, pp. 204-372).

men.[24] Many others fought in the sea-battles at the Hellespont,
b   seizing all the enemy's ships in one day and winning many other
encounters.[25] I said there was something terrible and unexpected
about the war: I meant that the rest of the Greeks came to desire
victory over our city so much that they dared to make a treaty
with our most hated enemy, the King, whom they and we in a
common effort had expelled; in private they entreated him to return, a Barbarian against Greeks, and they assembled against our
c   city all the Greeks and Barbarians.[26] Then, indeed, did the might

---

[24]   This is the literal sense of the Greek, if one takes *echein epainon* in the usual
way ("to be praised") together with "enemies" and "friends", which are
in the nominative. But the oddity of the suggestion that it is the Athenians' enemies who are being praised for their moderation and virtue, in
the context, has prompted Stallbaum, and Graves following him, to take
the lead of an accepted reading of *echein mempsin* ("to give blame") and
thus translate the Greek along the lines of "these men, who received more
praise for moderation and virtue from the very enemies who fought them
than other men receive from their friends." See Graves, *The "Euthyphro"
and "Menexenus" of Plato*, p. 108.

[25]   Socrates is referring to the Athenian victories at Cynossema, Cyzicus, and
Abydos (411-410 B.C.). He overstates somewhat the degree of Athenian
success in these engagements. The confrontation at Cynossema ended with
both the Athenians and Spartans taking about equal losses in men and
ships; it was a success insofar as it enabled the Athenians to sail through
the Hellespont. This allowed them to recapture Cyzicus, a city that had
revolted from the Athenians, and seize the eight ships docked there
(Hammond, *A History of Greece*, p. 410). These victories were less important for strategic purposes than for morale. At Abydos, the Athenians defeated the Spartan admiral Mindarus, who was killed in the fighting, and
destroyed or captured his entire fleet. In the wake of the disastrous defeat
in Sicily, it showed that the Athenians were still capable of besting the
Spartans at sea (Grote, *History of Greece*, vol. 8, pp. 97-107; Thucydides
VIII.104-6).

[26]   In 413 B.C. the Spartans and Persians began to collaborate against Athenian interests in Ionia. The Persians, intent on reclaiming the cities of Ionia,
agreed to cover the military expenses of the Spartans if they in turn would
aid the revolt in Chios. Both worked in conjunction to take the Ionian
cities away from Athens. The agreement between them, known as the
Treaty of Miletus (412 B.C.), was that all Greek colonies originally belong-
ing to Persia would be returned to the Persian empire (Thucydides VIII.18).
This treaty was made immediately after the Milesians, aided by the Spartans and by Alcibiades, revolted against and overthrew their pro-Athe-
nian government. Contrary to Socrates' claims, though, the Spartans were
hardly entreating the Persians to return to Greece, and the treaty did not
last long. In the summer of 412, it was dissolved, as the Spartans expressed
their fears that the agreement would allow the Persians to reclaim Thessaly
and Boeotia and ultimately make the Persians masters of the Greeks
(Thucydides VIII.37, 43; Grote, *History of Greece*, vol. 7, pp. 385-415; Fine,
*The Ancient Greeks*, p. 500).

and virtue of our city become manifest. For although she was thought to be already worn down by war and although her ships were taken at Mytilene, men came to the rescue in sixty ships; these men, who embarked of their own accord, came to be acknowledged as best since they conquered their enemies and freed their friends, though, having obtained an unworthy fortune as they were not recovered from the sea, they now lie there.[27] It is

d    right always to remember and praise them, for by their virtue we won not only that sea-battle but the rest of the war.

Indeed, because of them our city gained the reputation that it would never be overcome in war, not even by all humanity. And this proved true—we were vanquished not by others but by our own discord. Even now we remain undefeated by others, but we have conquered and defeated ourselves. After the fighting, when

e    there was quiet and we were at peace with everyone else, we waged our own war at home in such a way that if in fact it should be fated for human beings to endure civil strife, no city would pray to suffer this disease differently.[28] For how readily and amicably did the citizens from the Piraeus and the town reconcile with one another and, contrary to expectations, with the other Greeks as well, and how equitably did they settle the war with

[27]    This is a reference to the battle of Arginusae (406 B.C.), the largest naval engagement of the Peloponnesian War. Although the outcome was an Athenian victory, a severe storm prevented the Athenians from rescuing the crews of damaged ships and recovering the bodies of the dead for burial. Of the eight surviving generals, two refused to return to Athens, and the remaining six were placed on trial for what was perceived as an egregious neglect of duty—the failure to recover the bodies of the Athenian dead. They were found guilty and sentenced to death. Among the six was the younger Pericles, Aspasia's son. That the six generals were tried as a group was a clear transgression of Athenian legal procedures. For this reason, Socrates refused to take part in the trial, after strenuously urging the council to try them in strict accordance with legal procedure (*Apology* 32b-c; Grote, *History of Greece*, vol. 8, pp. 152-186; Fine, *The Ancient Greeks*, pp. 513-14. For further details of the trial see Xenophon's *Hellenica* I.7.1-35).

[28]    In July of 404 B.C., Athenian oligarchs, supported by a show of force from the Spartan general Lysander, decreed that thirty men be elected to establish a constitution framed after the ancestral laws (Fine, *The Ancient Greeks*, p. 519). The Thirty limited the number of Athenian citizens to 3,000 and began a reign of terror that claimed 1,500 lives (Xenophon *Hellenica* II.3.11-21; Fine, *The Ancient Greeks*, p. 520; Grote, *History of Greece*, vol. 8, pp. 204-249). A group of exiles led by Thrasybulus eventually regained power (Summer of 403) and remarkably exacted no reprisals from the former oligarchs, as they instituted a strictly-enforced amnesty.

244a    those in Eleusis! There is no other explanation for all this than a
        true kinship, which secures, not in name but in fact, a friendship
        that is steady and of the same race. It is right to remember also
        those who died in this war at one another's hands, and, since we
        have become reconciled, to reconcile them as we are able, with
        prayers and sacrifices on occasions such as this, praying to those
        who rule over them. For not out of vice did they attack one an-
  b     other, nor out of enmity, but through misfortune. We, the living,
        ourselves bear witness to this, since we, who are of their race,
        have forgiven one another, both for what we did and for what we
        suffered.

        After this, when we were completely at peace, our city kept quiet.
        She pardoned the Barbarians for retaliating fully when they were
        suffering badly at our hands, though she remained vexed at the
        Greeks, remembering that they had returned the favor of being
  c     well treated by our city by joining the Barbarians, taking away
        our ships, the very ones which once had saved them, and taking
        down a wall in return for the walls of theirs we had prevented
        from falling. Our city thus carried on, deciding never again to
        fight against the enslavement of Greeks either by one another or
        by Barbarians. As we were in this frame of mind, the Spartans
        believed that we had fallen as the allies of freedom and that it
  d     was now at hand for them to enslave the others, and they set out
        to do so.[29] But what need is there to speak at length about this?
        For I would be speaking neither of ancient men nor of things that
        happened long ago. Indeed, we ourselves know how the fore-
        most of the Greeks—Argives, Boeotians, and Corinthians—came
        to our city in need, having been frightened out of their senses,
        and how, the most divine thing of all, even the King fell into such
        straits that he turned for protection to nowhere other than that
  e     very city he had so eagerly tried to destroy. In general, if some-

---

[29]   Socrates is now speaking of events that took place after his death in 399
       B.C. Athens was not "completely at peace" during the period immedi-
       ately following the Peloponnesian War. The absence of Athenian influ-
       ence in the Aegean left a power vacuum that was quickly filled by the
       Spartans. A dispute over the control of the Ionian cities led to open con-
       flict between the Spartans and Persians in 400. In the naval struggles that
       followed, many Athenian mercenaries joined the Persian fleet. As early as
       396 Athens was unofficially sending crews and arms to the Persian fleet.
       Open hostility erupted with the Spartans in 395 when the Athenians in-
       tervened on behalf of the Thebans to prevent a Spartan invasion of Boeotia.
       This was the beginning of the Corinthian War, much of which took place
       on the isthmus between the Peloponnese and central Greece (Grote, *His-
       tory of Greece*, vol. 9, pp. 346-361; Fine, *The Ancient Greeks*, pp. 542-548).

one should wish to accuse our city justly, only by saying this would he accuse correctly: that she is always too given to pity and a servant of the weak. Even in this instance, she was unable to be steadfast or to maintain her resolution no longer to help anyone who was enslaved against those who had done them an injus-

245a    tice; instead, she bent and helped. She helped the Greeks herself and freed them from slavery, so that they were free until they enslaved themselves again. But she did not dare to help the King, being ashamed before the trophies at Marathon, Salamis, and Plataea—although admittedly she saved him too by allowing fugitives and volunteers to help.

b    After building walls and ships, and entering the war since she was forced to do so, our city fought the Spartans on behalf of the Parians.[30] But the King began to fear our city when he saw the Spartans giving up in the war at sea. He wanted to withdraw, and so, as a condition of allying with us and our other allies, he demanded the surrender of the Greeks on the Continent, the same ones the Spartans had previously given to him. He believed that we would be unwilling to accept this and that he would thus have a pretext

c    for his withdrawal.[31] But he misjudged the other allies. For they were willing—the Corinthians, Argives, Boeotians, and the others agreed, swearing an oath that if the King were to give them money, they would hand over the Greeks on the Continent. We alone did not dare to give them up or to swear this oath. As you well know, the nobility and freedom of our city are this firm and sound, and we are by nature Barbarian-hating because, unmixed with Barbar-

d    ians, we are purely Greek. There live among us none of the descendants of Pelops, or Cadmus, or Egyptus, or Danaus, nor the many others who are Greeks by convention but Barbarians by nature. Rather, Greeks through and through, we live unmixed with Barbarians, which has given our city its pure hatred of foreign na-

---

[30]    There is no known war on behalf of the Parians (Graves, *The "Euthyphro" and "Menexenus" of Plato*, p. 111). A number of editors have thus suggested alternative readings to "Parians," including "Persians" (Graves), "Corinthians" (Stallbaum), and "Argives" (Hermann).

[31]    The resurgence of Athenian military might have induced the Spartans to make peace with Persia (392 B.C). They agreed to return the islands that once belonged to Persia and to allow the other Greek cities to remain free and autonomous. The Athenians and Thebans were opposed to this arrangement—the Athenians feared they would lose their recent acquisitions (Scyros, Imbros, and Lemnos). No decision was reached, and the Corinthian War continued for five more years (Xenophon *Hellenica* IV.8.12-17; Grote, *History of Greece*, vol. 9, pp. 413-415).

e  tures. So, since we were unwilling to perform the shameful and unholy act of giving away Greeks to Barbarians, we were once again deserted. Having fallen, then, into the same straits that had worn us down before, with the help of a god we brought the war to a better conclusion this time. For we escaped the war with our ships, our walls, and our colonies, since our enemies were glad to escape it as well.[32] Yet in this war too we lost good men, the ones who met

246a  rough terrain at Corinth and treachery at Lechaeum. And good also were those men who freed the King and drove the Spartans from the sea.[33] I recall them to you, but it is fitting that you too praise and honor such men.

Thus, about the deeds of the men lying here and of all the others who have died on behalf of our city, many noble things have been said. But things still more numerous and more noble are left to be

b  said; many days and nights would not be enough for one to cover everything. So it is right for every man who remembers their deeds to exhort the children of these men, just as in war, not to leave the post of their ancestors or fall back and yield to vice. And indeed, children of good men, I myself now exhort you, and whenever I

c  meet one of you in the future, I shall remind you and urge you to strive eagerly to be as good as possible. But on this occasion, it is just that I tell you what your fathers, as they were about to risk their lives, solemnly enjoined us to announce, should anything happen to them, to those whom they would forever leave behind. I declare to you both what I heard straight from them and,

---

[32]  A strong alliance was formed between Athens, Cyprus, and Egypt in 388 B.C. This concentration of power convinced the Persians that a friendly change of policy was needed toward Sparta. The Persians made a pact with the Spartans, and together they began to pressure the Athenians to accept the conditions of the treaty by effecting a complete blockade of the Hellespont and raiding the Attic coast. Upon accepting the terms of the treaty, the Athenians were allowed to keep Lemnos, Imbros, and Scyros. The accord went by several different names: the Peace of Antalcidas, the King's Peace, and the Common Peace (386 B.C.) (Grote, *History of Greece*, vol. 9, 432-438; Fine, *The Ancient Greeks*, p. 555).

[33]  The treachery Socrates speaks of in the preceding sentence took place in 392 B.C. when the long walls leading from Corinth to Lechaeum on the Gulf of Corinth were betrayed by oligarchic sympathizers within Corinth (Hammond, *A History of Greece*, p. 459). This enabled the Spartans to establish fortifications in northern Corinthia. Those who "freed the King" were the Athenian mercenaries who fought in the Persian fleet. The most notable of these was Connon, who fought successfully against the Spartan fleet on many occasions; the most renowned of his victories was at Cnidos in 394 B.C. (Grote, *History of Greece*, vol. 9, pp. 342-345, 383-395).

inferring from what they said then, what they would gladly say to you now if they had the power. But you ought to believe that what I am reporting, you are hearing straight from them. These are the things they said:

d     "Children, that you are of good fathers, the present now testifies. Though we could have lived ignobly, we instead choose nobly to die, before bringing you and your descendants into disgrace and before shaming our fathers and all our ancestors. For we believe that life is not worth living for the one who brings shame upon his own, and that such a man will find no friend among either human beings or gods, neither on the earth nor under it once he has died. Hence, it is right that you remember our speech, and even if you should practice something else, practice it with vir-

e     tue, knowing that without this all possessions and pursuits are shameful and base. For when coupled with unmanliness wealth does not bestow nobility upon its possessor: such a man is rich for another, not for himself. And beauty and strength of the body when joined with cowardice and vice do not appear seemly but unseemly, and they make the one who has them more conspicu-ous and reveal his cowardice. All knowledge, too, when severed

247a     from justice and the rest of virtue, reveals itself as villainy, not wisdom. For these reasons, try to be zealous—first and last, in all things and in every way—such that in the best case you may ex-ceed in renown both us and those who came before. But if you do not, if we surpass you in virtue, know that our victory brings us shame, whereas our defeat, should we be defeated, brings us hap-piness. What would be best, we would be defeated and you would be victorious if you should make sure that you do not abuse or

b     squander the reputation of your ancestors, knowing that for a man who believes himself to be something, nothing is more shameful than to allow himself to be honored not for his own worth but for his ancestors' reputation. The honors of parents are a noble and magnificent treasure for their descendants, but to spend a treasure of money and honors, failing to pass it down to one's descendants due to a lack of possessions and a good repu-tation of one's own, is shameful and unmanly. If you live by what

c     we have said, you will come to us as friends to friends when your own fate carries you off. But if you are neglectful and live basely, no one will welcome you favorably. To the children, then, let these things be said."

"As for our fathers and mothers, those of us who still have them ought always to urge them to bear as easily as possible whatever

d calamity should occur, and we ought not to join them in lamenting. They will not be in need of added grief as this misfortune will provide grief enough. Rather, healing and soothing them, we ought to remind them that of those things for which they prayed, the gods have given ear to the greatest. After all, they prayed not that their children become immortal, but that they become good and illustrious, and these, which are the greatest of goods, they obtained. For a mortal man, though, it is not easy for everything in his life to turn out as he intends. And yet by bearing the calamities courageously, they will be thought truly to be fathers of courageous children and themselves such as well; by yielding to their
e grief, however, they will arouse a suspicion either that they are not our fathers or that those who praise us lie. Neither of these suspicions ought to be aroused, but they most of all must praise us with deeds, showing themselves to be truly men who are fathers of men. The old saying "Nothing too much" certainly seems to be nobly said, and it is in fact well said. For if a man depends on himself for
248a everything or nearly everything that brings happiness and does not depend on other human beings, upon whose doing well or badly his own fortunes would be compelled to wander, he is the one who is best prepared to live. This man is the moderate one, and so also the courageous and prudent one. When his wealth and children come into being and perish, then most of all will this man obey the proverb, for since he relies on himself, he will be found neither taking joy nor grieving too much. We, for our part, esteem
b such men and wish and declare our own kin to be of this sort; and we now present ourselves as such too, not being excessively distressed or afraid if we must meet our end in the present circumstances. Indeed, we ask both our fathers and our mothers to spend the rest of their lives possessed of this same mind and to know that they will gratify us most neither by wailing nor by mourning over
c us. Rather, if there is any perception of the living by the dead, they would gratify us least by treating themselves badly and bearing the calamity grievously, and most by mourning lightly and with measure. As for our own lives, they have already come to an end, the very end which is noblest for human beings, so it is more fitting to honor what we have done than to mourn. And by caring for and nurturing our wives and children, turning their attention there,
d not only would our parents best be able to forget our fortune, but they would live more nobly and correctly, and would show us greater love. This is a sufficient message, then, from us to our families."

"To the city, we would make the exhortation that they take care of our parents and sons, giving the ones a well-ordered education and nursing the others properly in their old age. But of course we know that even without our making this exhortation, the city will take adequate care."

e

These are the messages, children and parents of those who have died, that these men solemnly enjoined us to relay, and I relay them as zealously as I can. And I myself, on their behalf, beseech you, the children, that you imitate your fathers; the parents, that you be heartened about your own welfare, since we will nurse you in your old age and care for you privately and publicly, whenever any of us happens to meet any of you. Of the care provided by the city, you yourselves surely know that the city makes laws regarding the children and parents of those who have died, and that to keep their fathers and mothers from being wronged, it has

249a

been ordered by the greatest authority that they be watched over more than the rest of the citizens. As for the children, the city herself shares in their rearing, eager that their orphanhood hardly be noticed by them, and she makes herself into the figure of a father while they are still young. When they reach manhood, she exhibits and recalls the pursuits of their fathers by providing the instruments of their patrimonial virtue and sends them forth to their inheritance arrayed in full armor; she sends them, under

b

the grace of an omen, to begin ruling in the house of their fathers, ruling with strength since they have been adorned with weapons. And she never fails to honor those who have died, each year performing in common for all those customary rites performed also in private for each. In addition to this, she establishes every manner of gymnastic, equestrian, and musical contest, and since

c

fate has cast her without design into the role of an heir and a son to those who have died—into a father to their sons and a guardian to their parents—our city takes complete care of all at all times. Taking these things to heart, you ought to bear the calamity more gently, for by doing so you would most endear yourself to the dead as well as to the living, and you would most easily heal others and be healed yourselves.

But now that you and all the others have completed the public lament of the dead, as is the law, depart."

d

There you have it, Menexenus, the speech of Aspasia the Milesian.

*Menexenus.* By Zeus, Socrates, this Aspasia you speak of must be blessed if, though a woman, she is able to compose such a speech.

*Socrates.* But if you don't believe me, come along with me, and you can hear her speaking.

*Menexenus.* I have run across Aspasia many times, Socrates, and I know what sort she is.

*Socrates.* What then? Don't you admire her, and aren't you now grateful to her for the speech?

*Menexenus.* Very much so, Socrates. I'm very grateful to her or to whoever else told you this speech. And most of all I'm grateful to the one who recited it.

*Socrates.* Fine. But make sure that you don't report me, so that I may continue to relay to you her many fine political speeches.

*Menexenus.* Be assured, I won't report you. Just relay them.

*Socrates.* This shall be done.